Oh, What a Loansome Time I Had

Oh, What a Loansome Time I Had

*The Civil War Letters of
Major William Morel Moxley,
Eighteenth Alabama Infantry,
and Emily Beck Moxley*

Edited by THOMAS W. CUTRER

THE UNIVERSITY OF ALABAMA PRESS
Tuscaloosa and London

Copyright © 2002
The University of Alabama Press
Tuscaloosa, Alabama 35487-0380
All rights reserved
Manufactured in the United States of America

9 8 7 6 5 4 3 2 1
10 09 08 07 06 05 04 03 02
The maps on pages 15, 39, 49, 65, and 132 were prepared by Susan Young.
The Moxley family tree was prepared by Karyn Jo Walsh.

Typeface is Adobe Caslon

∞

The paper on which this book is printed meets the minimum requirements of
American National Standard for Information Science–Permanence of Paper for
Printed Library Materials, ANSI Z39.48–1984.

Library of Congress Cataloging-in-Publication Data

Moxley, William Morel, d. 1878.
   Oh, what a loansome time I had : the Civil War letters of Major William Morel
Moxley, Eighteenth Alabama Infantry, and Emily Beck Moxley/ edited by Thomas W.
Cutrer.
      p. cm.
Includes bibliographical references and index.
ISBN 0-8173-1118-1
1. Moxley, William Morel, d. 1878—Correspondence. 2. Confederate States of America.
Army. Alabama Infantry Regiment, 18th. 3. Alabama—History—Civil War, 1861–1865—
Personal narratives. 4. United States—History—Civil War, 1861–1865—Personal narra-
tives, Confederate. 5. Alabama—History—Civil War, 1861–1865—Regimental histories.
6. United States—History—Civil War, 1861–1865—Regimental histories. 7. Soldiers—
Alabama—Correspondence. 8. Moxley, Emily Beck—Correspondence. 9. Moxley family
—Correspondence. 10. Coffee County (Ala.)—Biography. I. Moxley, Emily Beck.
II. Cutrer, Thomas W. III. Title.
   E551.5 18th .M68 2002
   973.7′82—dc21
                           2001004114

British Library Cataloguing-in-Publication Data available

For

my grandmother,
Quinnie Evelyn Cutrer

my mother,
Wilkie Lee Forrest

my wife,
Emily Martin Fourmy

my daughter,
Katherine Martin Cutrer

Four generations of Southern women

Nor Mars his sword nor war's quick fire shall burn
The living record of your memory

Contents

Figures

Acknowledgments

"The William M. Moxley Papers, 1854–1901," as the collection is officially catalogued, were donated to the Center for American History at the University of Texas at Austin, where they are now housed, on 30 January 1992 by Moxley descendents Frances Luccous of Houston, Texas, and Sarah Hagelstein of Midland, Texas. Numerous other individuals and institutions, as well as Mrs. Luccous and Mrs. Hagelstein, were generous in sharing with us information on the people, places, and events mentioned in the Moxley letters. The editors gratefully acknowledge the kindness of Katherine Adams, assistant director of the University of Texas Barker Texas History Center, for her vital assistance in obtaining copies of the Moxley letters; Donlay E. Brice, supervisor of Reference Services, Texas State Department of Archives, for assistance in tracing the Moxleys in Texas; Karen C. Bullard, genealogy librarian, Troy Public Library, for cheerful and expert guidance in Pike County lore; Henry Harken, associate librarian, Fletcher Library, Arizona State University West, for expert assistance in locating a number of rare and out-of-print documents; Jack M. Herchold of Pediatrix of Phoenix for help with obsolete medical terms and procedures; Kenneth W. Jones, university librarian, Dick Smith Library, Tarleton State University, Stephenville, Texas, for providing information on Confederate Alabama; T. Michael Parrish, archivist, Lyndon B. Johnson Library, for his unfailing willingness to share his copious knowledge of Civil War facts and sources; and Andy Phydas, military research archivist, Georgia Department of Archives and History, for information regarding Georgia in the Confederacy.

Most of all, I would like to acknowledge the vital assistance of Karyn Jo Walsh. Ms. Walsh and I began work on the Moxley papers in November 1998 as the capstone project of her bachelor's degree in American studies at Arizona State University West. She did the initial transcription of the letters and—as an expert genealogist—not only reconstructed the Moxley family tree but also taught me a great deal about the art and science of genealogic research, especially regarding sources on-line. Ms. Walsh successfully completed her degree in 1999, and she and her husband, Todd, are now the parents of two beautiful children, Tristan and Ireland.

Oh, What a Loansome Time I Had

Introduction

"Times are as hard here as mill Rocks," wrote Joseph H. Justice to his friend William M. Moxley on 12 January 1862. Indeed, the first year of the Civil War had laid a heavy hand on southeast Alabama, taking into the army men many of whom were not to return, introducing to home communities disease and privation that they had never before experienced, and causing local economies to stagnate. The collected letters of the extended Moxley family and many of their friends and neighbors make it distressingly clear exactly how hard times were in the Wiregrass during the year following Alabama's secession.

The Moxleys were typical of the yeoman-class farmers who constituted the bone and sinew of the Confederate heartland. William Morel Moxley, a physician and small farmer in Bullock, Coffee County, Alabama, was born in Burke County, Georgia in about 1824, the eldest son of Nathaniel and Jane (Matthews) Moxley.[1] Like many other early

---

1. Nathaniel Moxley was born in Virginia in or about 1760. He was the son of Joseph Moxley, an English-born Virginian, and his wife, whose maiden name was Dassey. Nathaniel's two older brothers, Benjamin and Daniel Moxley, were veterans of the American Revolution. Jane Matthews was born in North Carolina in or about 1787, the daughter of Aquilla Matthews. Both died in Louisville, Jefferson County, Georgia, in 1849. *Memorial Record of Alabama*, 788–789.

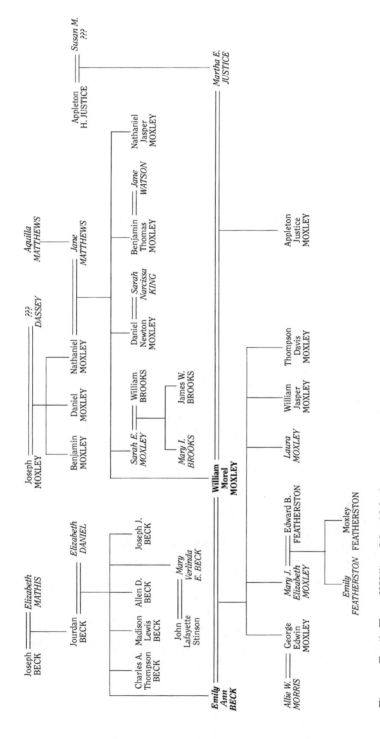

Figure 1. Family Tree of William Morel Moxley

nineteenth-century Southern families, the Moxleys followed the frontier, moving from Burke to Stewart to Jefferson to Henry County by 1850. All of these locations were, at the time, still very much a part of the Old Southwest frontier. Jefferson, for example, was described in the 1850 census as a county with zero libraries and fourteen churches—eight Methodist, one Presbyterian, four Baptist, and one "Hard Shell."[2] From Henry County in central Georgia, the Moxleys moved for a brief period to Barbour County in southeast Alabama before purchasing, on 4 November 1854, a forty-acre tract in northwest Coffee County, near the village of Bullock.

Where and how William Moxley received his medical training cannot now be determined, and he was perhaps only what was commonly called an "empiric," one who practiced medicine without benefit of formal education. In every Southern state except Louisiana, medical licensing virtually disappeared during the 1830s. With the wave of anti-elitism that swept the country during the Jacksonian era, medical historian Sally G. McMillen states, "any white man could declare himself a doctor."[3] From 1857 thorough 1858, however, William Moxley's younger brother was a student at the Reform Medical College in Macon, Georgia, and he might well have attended the same institution at the same time. By 1860 Moxley owned $1,000 in real property in Coffee County and $700 in personal property, making him fairly affluent by the standards of the place but by no means a member of the planter elite.

William Moxley had three brothers and one sister. Daniel Newton Moxley was born in Burke County, Georgia, on 12 May 1827. In 1850 he was living in Louisville, Georgia, with his sister, Sarah, her daughter, Mary I. Brooks, and her son, James W. Brooks. In 1855 he was reading medicine in Florida, and from 1857 thorough 1858 he was a student at the Reform Medical College in Macon, Georgia. By 1859 he was practicing medicine in New Providence, Alabama, with assets totaling $2,520 in real estate and $375 in personal property. He briefly commanded Company B, Twenty-fifth Alabama Infantry, but resigned after the battle of Shiloh because of ill health. On 20 October 1864 he mar-

2. Social Statistics, Jefferson County, Alabama, Seventh Census, 1850.
3. McMillen, *Motherhood in the Old South*, 14.

ried Sarah Narcissa King (12 November 1839–26 January 1926), a schoolteacher at New Providence. Daniel Newton Moxley died on 29 January 1901 and is buried beside his wife and children in the Providence Cemetery, one mile north of the Crenshaw County village of Glenwood.

Benjamin Thomas Moxley was born in or about 1832. On 29 December 1850 he married Jane Watson in Jefferson County, Georgia, where, in 1860, he was employed as a bricklayer. He served briefly as a private in Company C, Twentieth Georgia Infantry, before transferring to William Morel Moxley's company. He died in or about 1890.

Little is known of the fourth of the brothers, Nathaniel Jasper Moxley. He is reported to have served in a regiment of Georgia cavalry during the war, and as late as 1890 he was living in Augusta, Georgia.

Their sister, Sarah E. Moxley Brooks, was also a native of Burke County. In July 1860 she was residing in the home of her cousin, Martha A. Cheatham, in Louisville, Jefferson County, Georgia. She was thirty-four years of age at the time, the widow of William Brooks, and employed as a seamstress.

William's wife, Emily Ann M. Beck, was born on 16 March 1836 in Talbot County, Georgia, the daughter of Jourdan and Elizabeth Daniel Beck. Jourdan Beck was born on 9 September 1806 in Barnwell, South Carolina, the son of Joseph and Elizabeth (Mathis) Beck. Elizabeth Daniel Beck, known to her husband as Betsey, was born in Burke County, Georgia, on 28 April 1810. In 1850, Jourdan and Elizabeth Beck were farming in Muscogee County, Georgia, on a farm valued at $1,500. On 6 February 1857, they purchased one quarter section of land in the southwest corner of Pike County, Alabama, a mile east of the hamlet of Fleetwood and some two miles south of Henderson, or Henderson's Store, as it was then sometimes called.

Emily was the oldest of the six surviving children. Her younger siblings were Charles A. Thompson (Tom) Beck, who was born in December 1837; Madison Lewis (Mat) Beck, born in about 1840; Allen D. Beck, born in or about 1842; Mary Verlinda E. (Sis) Beck, born 21 April 1843; and Joseph J. Beck, born on 12 December 1849. The two youngest of these siblings were born in Muscogee County, Georgia.

Madison Lewis Beck became a farmer in Pike County and was the owner of one female slave, aged eighteen. On 13 January 1859 he married

Mary M. Stringer, daughter of Wilson B. Stringer and Margaret Ann (Williamson) Stringer.

On 18 January 1859, Mary Verlinda E. Beck was married to John Lafayette (Fate) Stinson who—like her brothers Mat and Tom—was to serve as a private in Company B, Twenty-fifth Alabama Infantry.

William and Emily were married on 15 September 1853 in Jefferson County, Georgia. Their first child, George Edwin Moxley, was born in Georgia on 31 December 1852, when Emily was about seventeen years old. Their next child, Mary J. Elizabeth Moxley, named after her grandmother but called Betty by her family, was born shortly before the Moxleys left Georgia in about 1855. Laura Moxley was born about a year later in Alabama in 1856. William Jasper Moxley, also called Willie, was born in about 1858 and was followed by Davis Moxley (later renamed Thompson, after his late uncle, Charles A. Thompson Beck) in 1860. Emily was pregnant with their last child as William entered the Confederate army in 1861.

Also prominent in the Moxley correspondence are the Stinson, Stringer, and Justice families. Robert M. Stinson, son of John and Martha C. Stinson, was twenty-three years old in 1860 and serving as overseer on his father's farm. He was the husband of Emily Moxley's cousin Emiline E. Stinson, and with his brothers John Lafayette and Micajah Jason, he enlisted in Company B, Twenty-fifth Alabama Infantry, as did their cousin Elias Green Stinson, the son of the Beck's nearest neighbors, Micajah B. and Sarah J. Stinson. John B. Stringer, Mat Beck's brother-in-law and the son of Wilson Baker Stringer and Margaret Ann (Williamson) Stringer, served as a private in the same company.

Appleton H. Justice, a Coffee County merchant, was forty years old in 1860. Locally prominent, Justice was elected a county commissioner on 6 May 1861 and served as postmaster at Bullock from 5 March 1860 through 18 July 1866 except during a period of military service at Pensacola, Florida. Justice was in the army only briefly, however, before resigning due to ill health. He was married to Susan M. Justice.

Their son, Dawson W. Justice, a twenty-year-old clerk in 1860, was at that time living with the family of Thomas Wasden in Bullock. He enlisted in the Bullock Guards in June 1861 and by November 1861 had been elected sergeant major of the Eighteenth Alabama. He was reported wounded in action in the campaign for Atlanta at some time between 7 May and 4 June 1864.[4]

These parents and siblings and an extended family of in-laws and neighbors corresponded extensively with William and Emily Moxley, adding a depth and breadth of context and content to our understanding of the lives of these farm families struggling with the exigencies of war.

William Moxley's letters to his wife and to other members of his family offer insight into the daily life of a newly elected company-grade officer attempting to learn the art of war and to teach it to a group of enthusiastic but highly undisciplined volunteers. Issues of crime and punishment in camp; complaints about pay, mail service, food shortages, and inflated wartime prices; and rumors of battles lost and won and of an imminent peace dominate the news he sent home.

Alabama historian Leah Rawls Atkins has observed that the state's volunteers "were fighting for Southern independence in the spirit of the American Revolution, not to preserve property in slavery, which most of them did not own anyway."[5] This statement certainly seems true of William Moxley and his neighbors.

Coffee County was located in the so-called Wiregrass district of southeast Alabama, a region characterized by dense pine forests and barren sand or clay soils. The county and those surrounding it, therefore, were among the last frontier regions east of the Mississippi River. They were never part of the Cotton Kingdom and were never participants on a large scale in the plantation economy and its "peculiar institution." The region's agriculture was largely built on a subsistence base: peas, corn, and—following the Civil War—peanuts. In 1850, in fact, Coffee had 6,380 white inhabitants and only 557 slaves. By 1860 this frontier county had matured to the point where its 5,380 white inhabitants owned 1,417 bondsmen, but its red clay and piney woods character guaranteed that it would never rank with the great plantation districts of the Southern tidewater and river valleys.[6]

4. Pay and Muster Roll, Eighteenth Alabama Infantry, November 1861, Alabama Department of Archives and History; *Selma Morning Reporter* (Alabama), 16 June 1864.

5. Rogers et al., *Alabama*, 197.

6. Coffee County has the unique distinction of having erected a monument to that greatest of

Serving the Southern cause and suffering deprivation for neither slavery nor jingoistic patriotism, William and Emily Moxley nevertheless saw the North as the aggressor in the conflict, and both wrote of wanting nothing but the recognition of the Confederate States of America as an independent nation. William Moxley, unhappy in the army and longing for home, wrote to his wife that he could return only "when our Country is at peace and occupies a place among the nations of the Earth." "God grant that we may gain the victory and all can go home to their familiys and live in peace and comfort," was Emily Moxley's simple prayer.

William and Emily Moxley did not own slaves. Emily's father, Jourdan Beck, owned four: a man named Robin, who is mentioned in these letters with remarkable affection, and his wife and two children. The senior Beck writes of making less than two bales of cotton in 1861, apparently an average yield for his farm. Of the Moxleys' acquaintances, only Wilson Baker Stringer—the father-in-law of Emily's brother Mat —seems remotely to have approached the station of plantation aristocracy; he owned twelve slaves in 1850 and twenty-nine in 1860. In keeping with his planter status, Stringer was elected as one of Pike County's representatives to the Alabama state legislature in 1865 and 1866 before migrating to Texas. He was also a Primitive Baptist preacher.[7]

Perhaps because of their fragile link with the plantation South, the Moxleys' faith in ultimate Confederate triumph was not particularly strong, and their letters display remarkably little of the fervent patriotic rhetoric that characterizes much Civil War correspondence. Even this limited enthusiasm for cause and country declined as war went on. Although never critical of the Confederacy's goal of independence, Emily Moxley became increasingly disdainful of the management of the Southern war effort. Echoing her husband's observations and complaints of lack of patriotism—even in the Confederate officer corps— she offers her opinion that "if the officers of the present day were such men as the old revolutioners were, we would be more successfull in our battles." But the senior officers of her husband's regiment, she believed,

---

scourges to Southern cotton, the boll weevil. In appreciation for its role in bringing about the diversification of the region's agriculture, the marker on the grounds of the county courthouse at Enterprise identifies the insect pest as "the Herald of Prosperity."

7. Farmer, *One Hundred Fifty Years in Pike County, Alabama, 1821–1971*, 511.

were "in for money and do not think of the responsibility that rests upon there heads." If the leaders of the new Confederate nation were to "do as they should" and support their cause "with a pure motive and with a heart that can feel for there men that are under them," she wrote, "God would be with them unto the end."

She and her husband saw only corruption, greed, and personal ambition in high places, however, and so despaired of the ultimate victory. "When I see how much difference in the officers of the present day & the old Revolution," wrote William Moxley, "it does in some degree shake my faith in our success. There cannot be any simularity if Hystory gives us a correct an account." When the unfounded rumor of the fall of Savannah reached Coffee County on 24 February 1862, Emily Moxley was moved to write to her husband, "It seams that God has forsaken us," and when Nashville was actually captured on the following day, she wrote, "I see no chance for us now, or but very little, at least."

Although Emily Moxley was not typical of the "patriotic women of the Confederacy" to whom the Congress tendered its resolution of thanks on 9 April 1862 for "the energy, zeal, and untiring devotion which they have manifested in furnishing voluntary contributions to our soldiers in the field, and in the various military hospitals throughout the country," she, and her fellow women of the Wiregrass, were nevertheless subject to the horrors of America's first total war and made sacrifices to the Confederate cause as great as any offered by the nation's female elite.[8]

As interesting and valuable as William Moxley's commentary on the life of two company-grade officers are, and as revealing as are his and his wife's critique of the faltering Confederate cause, for the social historian the true worth of the Moxley letters lies in their domestic content. In her 1903 memoir, Nell Grey, the wife of Daniel Grey, adjutant of the Thirteenth Virginia Cavalry, observed, "Before the war, it was scarcely considered wise or delicate for women to live without the protection of a male relative in the house, and as far as possible they were shielded from the burden of business responsibilities."[9] Similarly, twenty-year-old Georgia plantation mistress Ella Gertrude Clanton

---

8. "Resolution of Thanks," First Congress, 9 April 1862, in Richardson, *A Compilation,* 1:231.
9. Avary, *A Virginia Girl in the Civil War,* 10–11.

Thomas jotted in her journal in 1855, "True to my sex, I delight *in looking up* and love to feel my woman's weakness protected by man's superior strength."[10]

This tradition of patriarchy died hard in the Wiregrass, as it did in the rest of the Confederacy as well, but the enforced absence of men thrust responsibility upon Southern women of all classes and delivered to them a degree of autonomy that they had never before experienced. In the spring of 1862 one Rebel cavalryman noted that "for the first time" he had seen "white women working in the field." They were "compelled to work," he wrote, "by reason of their male relatives being in the army," and so must themselves plow, sow, and harvest "or do without bread."[11]

Southern soldiers sought to rectify this imbalance by their sacrifices on the battlefield. "Even now we are endeavoring to repay them," wrote Robert Franklin Bunting, the chaplain of the Eighth Texas Cavalry, "in protecting their homes, defending their rights, and soon we hope to drive the foul invader and insulting foe from their State." Since the women of the South were "willing to make every sacrifice," he wrote, "why shall not we do our duty in their defence and for their deliverance?"[12]

Not surprisingly, however, despite these women's rapidly developing ability to carry out the responsibilities vacated by their men, absent husbands were reluctant to relinquish control of their property and families and attempted to supervise their wives by correspondence or by the proxy of a male relative.[13] William Moxley, a loving but traditional husband and father, offered direction to his wife on virtually every aspect of child raising, farming, and medical treatment but generally insisted that she rely upon the judgment and support of his manifestly incompetent or unconcerned brother at home. More important, her letters to him— among the pitifully few remaining collections of letters from wives to their soldier husbands—offer an almost unique chronicle of the loneliness, fear, and growing resourcefulness of a rural, yeoman-class wife, left to rely upon her own sagacity and strength to keep farm and family alive

10. Burr, *The Secret Eye*, 122.
11. *Houston Tri-Weekly Telegraph*, 25 July 1862.
12. *Houston Tri-Weekly Telegraph*, 14 January 1863.
13. Krug, "Women and War in the Confederacy," 415.

under conditions of unprecedented stress and deprivation. Emily Moxley's letters are not only rich in the reporting of such day-to-day concerns as the recovery of lost or stolen livestock, the payment and collection of debts, and the problems of buying shoes and blue jeans for a family of growing children as the Union blockade took effect but are especially compelling in their emotional content.

Although as early as the summer of 1861 the Huntsville, Alabama, *Democrat* was urging its female readers not to write "gloomy letters" to their relatives in uniform,[14] from the time her husband left home Emily Moxley fully expressed her anxiety and sense of abandonment as she was condemned to a life of isolation from family and friends while the surrounding community became increasing lawless and violent under the pressure of wartime displacement and privation and the absence of male protection.

As Drew Gilpin Faust has written, the white women of the South had been "socialized from an early age in the doctrines of paternalism with their implicit promises of reciprocal obligation." In common with other Southern women of all classes who lost their men to the War, Emily Moxley retained for months "the sense of a moral economy of gender" that had bartered her autonomy for the protective care of a husband or other male relative. "I have all ways had a dear Husband to provide for me and to [be] a head in every thing, and now I have no one that cares for my wellfare," she complains shortly after her husband's departure. Other early letters flatly assert her helplessness. "I am a dependent," she writes in September, and in October 1861, "I cant do any thing by my self." As the war progressed, however, she took charge of her own life, hesitantly at first, but with growing assurance, and began to announce her decisions to her husband rather than to ask his permission and beg his forgiveness for actions that might have been against his will.[15]

14. *Huntsville Democrat*, 21 August 1861.

15. Faust, "Altars of Sacrifice," 1220. Emily Moxley's fears of physical danger were by no means groundless. On 3 September 1863, the Coffee County courthouse at Elba was burned by maurauding deserters from the Confederate army. Seeking, of course, to destroy the record of their enlistments, they also vastly complicated the task of later researchers. For an account of wartime depredations in Coffee County, see Fleming, *Civil War and Reconstruction in Alabama*, 124. Also of value is McMillan, *The Disintegration of a Confederate State*. Among the best studies of Southern farm women and their experiences of the Civil War are Bleser, *In Joy and Sorrow;* Clinton and Silber, *Divided Houses;* Faust, *Mothers of Invention;* Fox-Genovese, *Within the Plantation;* and Krug, "Women

Her growing sense of independence and self-reliance did not, however, shield her from a burgeoning sense of despair, so that by the beginning of 1862 she was writing to her husband, "I hate to beg you so hard to do any thing, but I cant help it this time and be reconciled to my fate." After pleading with him to return home to attend the birth of their child, she concluded, "If you cant come, I hope God will be with me and bear me up in my troubles, and if we never meet in this wourld, I hope we may meet in a better wher parting will be no more." In this profundity of despondency, she exemplified Faust's observation that "wartime experiences rendered some women almost incapable of functioning" because of what she characterizes as traumatic stress reactions or severe depression.[16] With the continued absence of her husband, the deaths of a brother and a brother-in-law within a four-week period, the increasing difficulty in caring for her young family, and her own advanced pregnancy, it is not surprising that she lamented, "I dont feel like I could go through with what I shall have to bear."

Also of great interest and value in the Moxley letters is their wealth of commentary concerning the epidemics of disease that shattered both Southern armies and Southern home communities during the first year of the war. The Bullock Guards, like other volunteer companies throughout the South, was formed through enlistment from its local community. As a result, these men had grown up together, had worked, studied, worshiped, and played together, and were frequently related by birth or marriage. Fatalities, therefore, either in combat or, more commonly, from disease, struck rural counties particularly hard. This was certainly the case with Coffee and Pike. A remarkable number of the men of Company A, Eighteenth Alabama; Company B, Twenty-fifth Alabama; and of Company F, Thirty-third Alabama Infantry—all recruited from these two sparsely settled southeast Alabama counties— were related to or were very close acquaintants of the Moxley and Beck families.

William Moxley was a physician in civilian life, and his letters are a particularly rich repository of professionally informed observations on the health of volunteer soldiers brought together in large numbers and

and War in the Confederacy." For an examination of Alabama's female elite during the period of the war, see Clay-Clopton, *A Belle of the Fifties.* An older treatment of Confederate women, specific to Alabama, is Sterkx, *Partners in Rebellion.*

16. Faust, "Altars of Sacrifice," 1222.

unsanitary conditions. Having experienced minimal exposure to microbes and viruses while growing to adulthood on farms and in small towns, recruits had never acquired the immunities necessary to fight off even the most common of "childhood diseases" such as measles, mumps, and scarlet fever and so died by the tens of thousands. As Moxley wryly reported, "armies will be sick any where you may put them."

Equally important, and much less common in Civil War letters, are Emily Moxley's reports on the health of the civilian community, as hard hit by the contagion of "camp fevers" as were the armies. Her letters are replete with graphic descriptions of illnesses brought home from the camps by her kinsmen and neighbors and with the treatments offered by stunningly incompetent and ignorant medical practitioners. Deaths in the Moxley circle were numerous, and Emily's reports of the bereavement of surviving spouses and parents are simple, touching, and effective.

Her letters also leave a poignant record of a life-threatening medical condition that the soldiers were spared—the horror of childbirth in a preantiseptic era, especially at a time when the most respected physicians accompanied the army and expectant mothers were deprived of the moral support of husbands, also in military service.[17]

Although preoccupied with thoughts of disease and death, Emily Moxley continued to be sustained by her love of her husband—"You told me to comb my hair ever time I thought of you," she wrote to him. "That is out of my power, for I would do nothing but comb it, for there is not one minute in the day but what I think of you." Such a statement was typical of her affirmations of affection. She also exhibited strength of character: "No one knows my troubles but my self. . . . I keep mine to my self and do the best I can," she wrote to her husband at a time when she and her children were reduced almost to starvation. Another source of comfort was a deep and abiding religious faith. In every letter she called upon God to deliver her family and her country from the scourge of war, and when William Moxley was near death with camp

---

17. Donna Rebecca D. Krug notes in her survey of Southern women's "letters of hardship" to the Confederate war department that a significant percentage of the pleas for relief concerned the absence of physicians from civilian communities. Krug, "Women and War in the Confederacy," 424–425.

fever, she counseled him to "try and be prepared to meet Him in a wourld where sorrow and pain are felt and feard no more."

Despite Moxley's presumed level of education as a physician, his letters are seldom formally grammatical, and his spelling is often phonetic at best. Those of his wife are even farther from standard English, and those of many of their wartime correspondents are scarcely literate. The editors have chosen to leave them almost entirely as they were written, with all of their idiosyncrasies of spelling and syntax. We have, however, taken the liberty of providing punctuation—of which most originals were entirely innocent—and paragraph breaks. We have regularized the capitalization of days of the week and other proper names and have inserted in square brackets such words and occasional letters as might make the meaning clearer. Otherwise, the Moxley correspondence is transcribed as the editors found it.

All data regarding age, place of birth, and occupation given in the footnotes come from the 1860 federal census unless otherwise noted. Annotations regarding prominent military and political officers, military actions, units, and installations are, unless otherwise documented, drawn from such standard Civil War reference sources as Richard N. Current, ed., *Encyclopedia of the Confederacy;* Patricia L. Faust, ed., *Historical Times Illustrated Encyclopedia of the Civil War;* E. B. Long, *The Civil War Day by Day;* and Ezra Warner, *Generals in Gray.*

I

"For you and them I am willing to die"

10 June 1861–22 October 1861

The military duty that tore William Moxley from his home was typical for an officer of company grade and, later, of field grade in a volunteer regiment. Alabama seceded from the Union on 11 January 1861 and shortly thereafter became "the Cradle of the Confederacy." By October 1861, Governor Andrew Barry Moore had announced that "27,000 Alabamians were enrolled in twenty-eight regiments of infantry and one cavalry regiment," and by the end of the war an estimated 120,000 of the state's men had served the Confederacy in a total of sixty regiments of infantry, thirteen of cavalry, and six battalions and twenty batteries of artillery. Col. William Henry Fowler, Alabama's superintendent of army records, reported that his state had sent more men into military service than any other Southern state and that the men represented a greater percentage of the state's population; in fact, North Carolina held a better claim to this distinction.[1]

William Morel Moxley swelled the tide by helping to raise the Bullock Guards, Coffee County's first infantry company, of which he was elected captain on 4 July 1861.[2] Moxley received thirty-nine of the forty

1. Wheeler, *Alabama*, 39; Rogers et al., *Alabama*, 197; Fleming, *Civil War and Reconstruction in Alabama*, 78, 81.

2. Hand-written ballot return, Confederate Muster Rolls Collection, Alabama Department of Archives and History, Montgomery, Alabama.

Figure 2. Southeast Alabama, 1860 (map by Susan Young)

votes cast for company commander. Bowling W. Starke was elected first lieutenant with thirty-eight votes; Joseph H. Justice received thirty-eight votes for second lieutenant; and Samuel J. Pollard, thirty-six for third lieutenant. Joseph M. Harper was elected first sergeant, with sixteen votes to eleven for Joseph Blake and nine for W. J. Howell.

The Bull Pups, as they called themselves, became one of the "twenty companies from South and Middle Alabama" that Governor Moore accepted into state service on 21 July 1861. On 25 July, Moxley was ordered by the state's adjutant general to report with his company to Camp Johnson, Alabama's camp of instruction at Auburn in Macon County. According to Moxley's official report, however, his company had received the order on 15 July and accordingly "took up the line of march July 22," trudging the fifty-eight miles from Elba to Greenville in Butler County, "where transportation was furnished" to Auburn. There, Moxley's Bullock Guards became Company A of the Eighteenth Alabama Infantry.

The Eighteenth Alabama, recruited from Butler, Coffee, Coosa, Covington, Jefferson, Pike, Shelby, and Tuscaloosa Counties, was organized at Camp Johnson on 4 September and was mustered into Confederate service on 16 September by a special order from Adjutant and Inspector General Samuel Cooper.[3] The regiment's first field officers were Edward Courtney Bullock, colonel; Richard Freer Inge, lieutenant colonel; and James Thadeus Holtzclaw, major.[4]

Colonel Bullock, whom Pvt. Edgar W. Jones characterized as "the most genteel of gentlemen," was born 7 December 1822, graduated from Harvard University in 1842, and shortly thereafter moved to Eufaula, Alabama, from his native Charleston, South Carolina. There he practiced law until 1857 when he was elected to the first of his two terms in the state senate. With Alabama's secession he volunteered as a private in the Eufaula Rifles, First Alabama Infantry, but soon received his appointment from Governor Moore to be commander of the Eighteenth Alabama.[5]

Eli Sims Shorter, who was also a Eufaula attorney, was the second colonel of the Eighteenth Alabama and took command after Bullock's

---

3. William M. Moxley, "Record of Events," 7 August to 30 November 1861, Alabama Department of Archives and History; Special Orders Number 154, Adjutant and Inspector General's Office, Richmond, 16 September 1861; *The War of the Rebellion: A Compilation of the Official Records of the Union and Confederate Armies*, vol. 52, pt. 2, pp. 148–149. Henceforth the *Official Records* will be cited as *OR*. Unless otherwise noted, I refer throughout to series 1.

4. Jones, *History of the 18ᵗʰ Alabama Infantry Regiment*; J. M. Carroll, comp., *The Confederate Roll of Honor* (Bryan, Tex.: J. M. Carroll, 1985), 15.

5. Wheeler, *Alabama*, 504; Owen, *History of Alabama*, 3:255; Jones, *History of the 18ᵗʰ Alabama Infantry*.

death on 23 December 1861. Shorter led the regiment at Shiloh and Corinth but resigned from the army on 10 May 1862 because of ill health.[6]

The regiment's third colonel, James Thadeus Holtzclaw, was born in McDonough, Georgia, on 17 December 1833. He practiced law at Montgomery from 1855 until the outbreak of war, when he was elected a lieutenant of the Montgomery True Blues. In August 1861, Jefferson Davis appointed him major of the Eighteenth Alabama, and the following December he was promoted to lieutenant colonel. Although Holtzclaw was seriously wounded at Shiloh, he rejoined his regiment within ninety days and was promoted to colonel, with the promotion dating to the day of his wound.[7]

Back in Coffee County during the war's first summer, Emily Moxley was finding life difficult in the absence of her husband and brothers. Her corn and potatoes, she reported to William Moxley, "were eat out clean" during a brief absence from home, leaving her "nothing but some side meat and corn meal." She was without funds as well, having even "to borrow money to pay the postage on this letter," and worse, she lamented, "You cant imagin how loansome I am. It look like there is somebody's dead." "It is harde times," she concluded, "but I hope it will get better soon."

[*N. Jasper Moxley to William M. Moxley*]
June 10, 1861
Jeffison County, Ga.
W. M. Moxley

Dear Brother,

Your letter came to hand yesterday, whitch gave me mutch pleasure to hear from you & to hear you & family was well. This leave my self

6. Shorter had been elected to Congress as a Democrat in 1855 and in 1857 and remained active in politics until his death in 1879. Wheeler, *Alabama*, 801.

7. In the autumn of 1862, Holtzclaw was sent to Mobile in command of a brigade. After he had recovered from an injury sustained at Chickamauga, he was promoted to brigadier general and took command of Henry DeLamar Clayton's brigade, which he led at Lookout Mountain and Missionary Ridge, throughout the Atlanta campaign, and during Hood's invasion of Tennessee. In January 1865, Holtzclaw took command of the division that formed the garrison of Spanish Fort. Here for thirteen days—27 March–8 April 1864—2,700 Confederates held at bay 25,000 Federal troops. Holtzclaw was paroled at Meridian and returned to Montgomery to resume his law practice. He died 19 July 1893. Jones, *History of the 18th Alabama Infantry;* Wheeler, *Alabama*, 418.

& famly all well as common. I saw [Benjamin] Thomas [Moxley] on Saturday; he was well. I saw Jamas Cheatham[8] on Saturday. He said Sarah & Mary[9] was well. The connection is all well as far as I know.

You wrote that Waters was after you for the money you [went] security to for me. I have not got the money at the present. I have due notes on two men that is gone off to war. One note call for one hundred & forty four dollars & fifty cents. The other one call for one hundred twenty eight dollars. If they have the luck to return, I will get it. If not, I fear it doutfull. All they both have some propperty & is very cleaver family of people. When I get it I will try to settle the case.

Times very heard in this county. Corne is worth one dollar therty seven & half per bushel, but crops are very good in general. I have the best corne crope I ever had in my life. I believe my cotton is not so good. Very good wheat crops maid this county. I hope times will be better.

The Jeffeson Geardes[10] will leave Louisvill[e] on the 19 of this month.[11] Thomas & William Godoanes has join the compain. Jamas Cheatham has join. Willaim Moxley, a son of Cousin Eligh Moxley, has join. Edmon Thomson, Leven Tommey, and several others that you are aquainted [with] has all join. Cousin Joseph Parker's son, William [and] Cousin James Parker's son, Solmon, are gone to Virginna, Harper['s] Fer[r]y.[12]

8. James A. Cheatham was the son of William Moxley's cousin Martha. He enlisted as a private in Company C, Twentieth Georgia Infantry. Henderson, *Roster of the Confederate Soldiers of Georgia*, 2:787.

9. Sarah E. (Moxley) Brooks is William's sister. Mary I. Brooks, who would have been about eighteen in 1861, is Sarah's daughter.

10. A unit called the Jefferson Guards was mustered into the Confederate Army in May 1861 as Company C, Twentieth Georgia Infantry. As a component of Lt. Gen. James Longstreet's corps, it served in every major battle of the Army of Northern Virginia except Chancellorsville and took part in Longstreet's Chickamauga and Knoxville campaigns. William D. Smith was the regiment's first colonel, and Roger L. Gamble was Company C's first captain.

11. Louisville, Georgia, the seat of Jefferson County, is located forty miles southeast of Augusta and some seven miles north of the Georgia Central Railroad. The town lay directly in the path of William T. Sherman's notorious "march to the sea" and was occupied by Federal cavalry, 27 November 1864.

12. All of these individuals mustered into the Jefferson Guards on 14 June 1861. Pvt. Thomas Goodowns, who was born in Georgia in 1841, died in Jefferson County in December 1861. Pvt. William A. Goodowns served for the duration of the war and surrendered with his regiment on 9 April 1865. James A. Cheatham died at Manassas, Virginia, on 15 August 1861. William A. Moxley served as a private until the surrender at Appomattox. A William E. Moxley joined on the same day but died at Manassas on 23 August 1861. Pvt. James R. Parker last appeared on the company's muster roll for 30 April 1861, but Pvt. William R. Parker served through the Appomattox campaign. Henderson, *Roster of the Confederate Soldiers of Georgia*, 2:786–788.

I had a notion going a while back, but has give out going at the present. The big manidgers had junced up things so, I thought I['d] let them mess a while & sea how they com out before join[ing], if I [do] atall. Thomas ses he is not a going to join atall.[13]

I have nothing of interest to write at present. I thought Waters note was settle long a go. I left over two hundred dollars out west and heard that note was settle with a part of. I have not had the chance to get out there to sea about those things.

Mollie[14] joines me in sending our best wishes & respect [to] your self and famley. [Write to me as] soon as [you] get this, whitch I hope will reach you fast & find your self and famly enjoying good health. So fairewell.

Yours as ever,

N. J. Moxley

Excuse all bloches mistake & bad spelling for [*word illegible*] sake.

~

[*George Goldthwaite to William M. Moxley*]
Adjt. & Ins. Gen. Office, Ala.
Montgomery, 25 July 1861
Capt. W. M. Moxley

Sir,

Enclosed you have orders to march with your company to Auburn at which point you will encamp with nineteen other companies till further orders.[15]

Your company will have to provide enough cooked provisions to last until it gets to Auburn and for fear of accidents you had better take one day's over.

---

13. Nevertheless, on 14 June 1861, Benjamin Thomas Moxley enlisted as a private in the Jefferson Guards, Company C of the Twentieth Georgia Infantry. In the fall of 1861 he transferred to his brother's company at Huntsville and was promptly detached to relatively comfortable duty as an ambulance driver. This is but one instance of the apparent favoritism that William Moxley showed his friends and kinsmen—a habit that seems to have placed him in ill repute with his superiors in the regiment. Henderson, *Roster of the Confederate Soldiers of Georgia*, 2:787; Hospital Pay and Muster Roll, Eighteenth Alabama Infantry, 31 October 1862, Alabama Department of Archives and History.

14. Mollie was the wife of Jasper Moxley.

15. In addition to the Eighteenth, the Fourteenth, Thirty-seventh, Forty-fifth, and Forty-eighth Alabama Infantry Regiments received their basic military training at Auburn. Logue and Simms, *Auburn*, 16.

You will determine the route for yourself, but it is supposed that it will be by Greenville and from that point by RailRoad. You will have to get to Greenville if you take that route, the best way you can. I suppose the neighbors will furnish transportation. You will be sup[plied] with, tents, arms, and subsistence after you arrive at Auburn.

I must urge upon you the importance of starting just as early as possible after receipt of these orders, and also, of the necessity of advising me just as soon as you receive them.

> Very respecly
> * sent
> Geo. Goldthwaite[16]
> Adjt. & Ins. Gen., Ala.

~

[*George Goldthwaite to William M. Moxley*]
Adjt. & Ins. Gen. Office of Ala.
Montgomery
25 July 1861
Orders

Captain W. M. Moxley of the Bullock Guards, will within three days after the receipt of this order, take up the line of march with his company for Auburn, Macon County, Alabama, where the company will be encamped till further orders.

On arriving at Auburn, Captain Moxley will report to the Officer acting as Quarter Master at that point, who will assign the camping ground and prov. with subsistence.

Capt. Moxley will advise this office of the *exact* day he will start with his company and as near as possible the day he will arrive at Auburn.

> By order of the Governor.
> Geo. Goldthwaite
> Adjt. & Ins. Gen.

16. George Goldthwaite was appointed adjutant general of Alabama with the state's secession and served for three years. Prior to the war he had been a justice of the Alabama Supreme Court and after the war was reelected to the circuit court in 1866. He was elected to the Senate in 1870. Wheeler, *Alabama*, 793; Owen, *History of Alabama and Dictionary of Alabama Biography*, 3:672.

~

[*William M. Moxley to Emily Beck Moxley*]
Camp Johnson,
Aug. 22, 1861
E. A. Moxley

Dear Wife,

According to promise, I am in my tent seting on wheat straw ½ past 8 oclock writing to you. I will first comment where we parted in Tuschegee.[17] I walked to the corner and looked after you as long as I could see the carriage. Then I returned to the upper part of the Court Square, took a chair, and waited for the Gentleman who promised to carry me to Nautasulga,[18] which he did. We left about 12 oclock and he carried me to his house. He changed horses a carried me within 4 miles of Camp Johnson. Then I took it a foot for the Camp, at which place I arrived about 6 Oclock in the evening.

I am certain that Gentleman is a friend to the soldier. He sent us some corn, peas, & cabbage, which was thankfully received.

Night before last, a short time after dark though the moon was shining as bright as ever it did, [I heard] some holloring from the boys. At first I paid but little attention to it, but soon I heard fife & drum. Then I thought it was a company coming. The noise increased untill acceeding the noise you heard when the man rode out on [a fence?] Rail. Well, I became anxious to learn where they were from, but owing to the crowd that geathered a round I could not reach them untill the crowd was dispursed by the Office[r] of the day. I am certain there were 1200 men arround them, but soon I found out they were from Barber. The next thing I found some of my old aquaintance. I will give you the names of some of them. First, Columbus Reaves, George Dubose, Council Bushe's Oldest Son, Green Gubbs, Joe Parmer, Dr. Welborn, Henry Smith, and others of my old patrons.[19]

17. William Moxley apparently returned home on leave shortly after arriving with his company at Camp Johnson, and Emily Moxley seems to have accompanied her husband on his return to his camp of instruction.

18. Notasulga was ten miles west of Auburn on the Montgomery and West Point Rail Road.

19. These were men of Seale's Guards, Company G, Twenty-ninth Alabama Infantry. Louis Brown Bush (4 August 1843–24 October 1904), the oldest son of Council Vernon Bush (May 1817–December 1893) and Rebecca Bishop, was the company's second lieutenant. Christopher Columbus Reeves, eighteen in 1860, was the son of H. T. and Martha Reeves of Barbour County. He and John

Our Regiment will be full to morrow, but [we] see no more prospect of leaving now than when we first came.

Not much sickness. No bad sickness. I feel very well to night.

Tell Mat [Madison Lewis Beck] to write to me. You answer this as soon as you can, for it will afford me great satisfaction to hear from you & the children often. Give my best wishes to all Enquiring Friends.

Yours as ever,
W. M. Moxley

~

[*Emily Beck Moxley to William M. Moxley*]
Pike Co., Ala.
Sept. 1, 1861

My Dear Husband,

I now seat my self to write you a few lines to let you know that we are all well at present and I hope these lines may find you the same.

Well, I have just returned from the river,[20] and I am very tired, for I walked home. The Pike Company[21] is gone. They left this morning. I can tell you we had a trying time of it, but you can gess at that. You cant tell how I feel this morning. My Dear Husband and Brothers are gone. It seems to me that we are all nearly heart Broken. It nearly killed Allen to part with us this morning. He cried like a child, but I did not see Tom [Charles A. Thompson Beck] shed a tear, but I expect he felt the more. Allen says he never will get over not going with you. He done all he could do to get Tom off with him to go in your Company, so Pa says. He rather be with you than any body els.

You know not my feelings this morning. Oh, if I could just see you I would be so happy, but I shall have to submit to my fate. I went

---

S. Welborn were both sergeants. Joseph L. Parmer was one of the company's corporals, and George W. Dubose, Green Worthy J. Grubbs, Jr., and Henry Smith served as privates.

20. This is the Conecuh River, which becomes the Escambia River upon crossing into Florida. The Conecuh bisects Pike County northeast to southwest and flows three miles to the northwest of Bullock, Alabama. The villages of Henderson and Fleetwood are on the river's east side, and New Providence is on the west.

21. The Pike Guards, in which Emily Moxley's brothers Allen D. Beck and Charles A. Thompson Beck were privates, soon became Company B, Twenty-fifth Alabama Infantry. The regiment's first duty station was at Mobile under Brig. Gen. Adley Hogan Gladden. Wheeler, *Alabama*, 134.

home from here last Monday morning. I found all right except my corn and potatoes. They were eat out clean. Not a thing to be seen. The place does not look right. There is something wanting to make it look right. Oh, what a loansome time I had there this week. It looks like I can never stay there. You cant imagin how loansome I am. It look like there is somebody's dead, but I hope it will not be so long. I trust in providence for better.

The [Pike County] Company is gone without any money or only 40 dollars [and] no uniform. They found there own blankets. Newton [Moxley] made three days trying to borrow the money but failed. I saw him this morning. He is well. He says he going down to my house to morrow. I shall be glad to see him come, all though I have but little to eat. I have had nothing but some side meat and corn meal. [Appleton H.] Justice brought 1 ham from Greenville with him. It is harde times, but I hope it will get better soon. Justice says he will get me somthing as soon as he can. He told me if I needed any to let him know, but I do hate to be so dependent. It is not like haveing you to go to. I shall have to borrow money to pay the postage on this letter, but I hope for the better.

I bought 4 meat hogs from Tom [Beck] for 13 dollars, which I promised to pay as soon as possible. They will weigh 100 punds a piece. Newton told me to get them. Justice allso advise me to get them. Tom told me if I could get 10 dollars for him, it would do. I takes the not[e]s and told J[ustice] if he could spare the money I would give him notes to hold untill I could pay him back the money, but he said he could not spare it, so Tom had to leave with out any.

I hate his going off with out any money, for he could have sold the hogs to others for the cash, but for my sake he left with out it. You musst remember him. He left with only 1 dollar in his pocket. I am sorry for him becaus he had no money.

Well, it is now evening and I have gust eat a harty dinner of kid. I thought of you while I was eating and wished for you to help me eat it, but it was all in vain. My wishing done no good, but I hope the time will come when we can eat together and live to gether in peace.

I tried to get that q[ua]rt[er] of beaf that Mr. Tomme[22] borrowed from us before you went off, and he would not pay it. He said he had paid you for it, but I did not believe it, for I think you told me he had

---

22. Augustine or Augustus B. Tommy of Bullock was a thirty-six-year-old merchant and mechanic in 1860. He was a neighbor of Appleton H. Justice and apparently assumed his duties as county commissioner when Justice went into the army.

not paid it. I may be mistaken, but I don't think I am. I want you to write to me and let me know the strait of it, and I want to know how much salt Elis borrowed from us.[23] I sent to him for it the other day, and he sent 1 peck and let me know how much more salt is loaned out and who borrowed it, for I do not know any thing about it and I am needing of it bad.

I received a letter from you last Wednesday, and I was more than glad to hear from you for I was very uneasy about you for you was not well when I left you, but I hope this may find you well.

I must close, for I have wrote all that I can think of that would interest you and a great deal more, I expect, but if I could see you I could tell you a great deal more. I want you to write often, for it is a great satisfaction to me to read a letter from you. The children send their love to you, and Ma [Elizabeth Daniel Beck] sends her love to you and says she wants you to live a Christian and prepare for a better world than this. She says that is her weak prayer. Robin[24] sends howdy to you and says he thinks a heap of Mass William. He says I must write something for him ever time I write. Sis [Mary Verlinda E. (Beck) Stinson] sends her love to you. Her and Ma is in a great deal of trouble to day.

You must look over bad writing and spelling. You must receive a good portion of love and respects from one that thinks more of your wellfare than anyone els could do.

> Yours untill Death,
> Emily A. M. Moxley
> to W. M. Moxley

Pa has just returned from New Providence. He went that far with the company. He says if I had not wrote to you this week, he would. So you need not think hard of his not writing to you this time. He thinks there is no use in his writing now. He send[s] his love to you.

> So farewell for a while, goodbye.
> E. A. M. Moxley

23. Four men from Bullock named Ellis—James, John J., M. J., and W. C.—served in Company F, Thirty-third Alabama Infantry. For the definitive discussion of the importance of salt, see Ella Lonn, *Salt as a Factor in the Confederacy* (New York: W. Neale, 1933).

24. In 1860, Jourdan Beck owned four slaves, a thirty-year-old woman; a man, aged thirty; and two male children ages five and two. Robin is presumably the man. Slave Census for Pike County, 1860.

The Pike Company, in which Emily Moxley's brothers Allen D. Beck and Charles A. Thompson Beck enlisted as privates, was locally known as The Pike Guards. It was mustered into Confederate service at Mobile in December 1861, however, as Company B, Twenty-fifth Alabama Infantry. Recruited in Coffee, Pike, St. Clair, Talladega, Pickens, Shelby, Calhoun, and Randolph Counties, the regiment was formed by the consolidation of the First (John Q. Loomis's) and Sixth (William B. McClellan's) Alabama Infantry Battalions. It took part in every engagement of Army of Tennessee from Shiloh to Bennington. Its first colonel, John Q. Loomis, was succeeded by George Doherty Johnston, with whom the regiment was most closely identified. William B. McClellan served as the regiment's first lieutenant colonel and Daniel E. Huger as its first major.

Like the Eighteenth, the Twenty-fifth Alabama remained at Mobile under Brig. Gen. Adley Hogan Gladden until ordered to join the Army of Tennessee at Corinth in February 1862. By then, however, disease had reduced the regiment to only 305 effectives. At Shiloh, 6–7 April 1862, it suffered 15 killed and 75 wounded. Heavy casualties forced the regiment's consolidation with the Nineteenth, Twenty-second, Thirty-ninth, and Twenty-sixth–Fiftieth Alabama shortly before the surrender of the Army of Tennessee at Durham, North Carolina, 26 April 1865. Only seventy officers and men of the old Twenty-fifth were present for the surrender.[25]

[*William M. Moxley to Emily Beck Moxley*]
Camp Johnson,
Sept. 1st[, 1861]
E. A. M. Moxley

My dear wife,

It is a great blessing to those who have absent relatives & friends to be in possession of means of communication. By such a blessing we can communicate all our thoughts & desires, which is a great satisfaction to me. Nothing but your presence & to hear you talk [would be] prefable.

25. Wheeler, *Alabama*, 134.

I received a letter from you by mail this morning dated Sept. 1st. I was scarcly through reading of it before Mr. Jones[26] gave [me] another backed by A. H. Justice. To [my] utmost delight, I found on opening of it it was from my Emily. But I hope you will never say that my patience would become weary before geting through with your delight-ful letter. It had been 20 pages long I could [not] have been tired of 21.

I must go to the field. The Govenor[27] will be out this [afternoon] to review the troops. When I come back I will give you all the news I have.

My Dear Emily, by candle light I resume my seat to finish my epistle amid noise & confusion. I find nothing for my mind so salutary in effect as contemplating on the Object of my Effection. Dear Emily, I thought how often I have asked you to walk of an evening into the Guarden, but, Oh, when you think of those pleasant hours, or at least pleaseant to me, and you absent, it casts a shaddow over evry thing else. My Dear, we have parted before, but under differend circum-stances. You expect me to return because you did not think of naturel death, that is, from disease. Now you fear both. But, my dear, if I should be killed, never regret, for it would be the best legacy I could leave you & my children. As Col. Bullock stated to me day before yes-terday, he said if he could die as Bartow,[28] let him go, for it would be the best legacy he could leave his children.

I must tell you something of our Colonel. Well, day before yester-day our Col. came. There was an escort appointed. They gave me the right of the Col. Capt. Morris[29] the left. Others in the rear. Myself and

26. Wiley Jones (1838–9 February 1881) was a neighbor of the Moxleys and a private in Company A, Eighteenth Alabama. He is buried in the Beaverdam Church Cemetery in Coffee County.

27. A prominent planter, attorney, former member of the state legislature, and judge of the circuit court, Andrew Barry Moore was elected governor of Alabama in 1857. Although a moderate on the secession issue, Moore ordered the seizure of all Federal property in the state some days prior to the Alabama secession convention and subsequently supported the Jefferson Davis administration. Moore served for the constitutional maximum of four years and left office in December 1861 to be replaced by John Gill Shorter. McMillan, "Alabama," 15–40; Stewart, *The Governors of Alabama*, 97–100.

28. Bartow, a native of Savannah, Georgia, resigned from the U.S. House of Representatives to become the captain of Company B, Eighth Georgia Infantry. He was promoted to colonel of the regiment on 1 June 1861 and was killed at the head of his brigade on 21 July 1861 at the first battle of Manassas. His last words are said to have been, "They have killed me; but, boys, *never* give it up." Davis, *Battle at Bull Run*, 199.

29. No one named Morris seems to have served as a captain in the Eighteenth Alabama. An H. Lewis Morris of St. Clair County was later captain of Company D, Twenty-fifth Alabama. He

Capt. Morris procured two fine Grey horses & Carriage. Myself & Capt. Morris took the carriage with the Col. Others of the escort rode in the rear. The Regiment went to Auburn to meat him. He stood a few yards from the Regiment below, in which condition he gave us a speech which was very appropriate. I could not help shedding tears. All the Citizens was taken with our Col., and so it is with evry body else that know Col. Bullock.

Our review came off first rate. My Company has the right wing of the Regiment which is the most important of all other in Regiment.[30]

My Dear Emily, you stated your letter to me was watered with your tears. Well, our tears mingled for I could not help it, neither did try to help it. You say you look to the time when I, you, & the children will meat when our Country is at peace and occupies a place among the nations of the Earth. I look forward to the day when we will be happy togeather. I think I shall be as happy as is posible for mortal man to be. I shall nevr be happy as long as I am sepperated from you, but I expect to take you with me.

I shall go to Montgomery to morrow night. I think I shall send you money to bring you up. Come as soon as you can. If I get money enough, I intend to keep you up here as long as we stay. I want you to go with me. If I should be killed in battle I want you to be close enough to see that [I] died for you & my children. It is for you and thcm I live & for you & them I am willing to die. My dear, you may be statisfied you always have the first place in my heart, and my children next. I am anxious to see you. I think while I am writing this sentence you and the children may be talking about me. It now 8 Oclock. My Emily, come as soon as you can.

The health of the Camp is tolerable good except measlis. One of Capt. Hammer['s][31] Company died last Monday. They sent him home,

---

was wounded and captured at Murfreesboro, was exchanged, and was later wounded at New Hope and Franklin.

30. In line with the European practice of placing the elite grenadier and light companies at either end of the battalion, the flanks of a regiment in the line of battle came to be regarded as places of honor and special responsibility. Although this tactical formation made some sense on an eighteenth-century battlefield, which was dominated by the smoothbore musket and the bayonet, it became a fossil in the age of the rifle. Haythornthwaite, *The Armies of Wellington,* 77.

31. William L. Hammer of Pike County was the first captain of Company H, Eighteenth Alabama Infantry, the "A. B. Moore Invincibles." He was promoted to surgeon and was replaced by Sheppard Ruffin. Hammer resigned as surgeon in November 1862, to be replaced by Dr. J. R. Barnett.

which they should have done. I think when it is a request they should comply. I wish I could meet you in Montgomery to morrow but I cant. I shall look for you soon.

I must close. Hug & kiss all the children for me. Tell them I think of them often, which I do. I have been happy, my darling, with you & them several times. Give my best wishes to all my relatives & friends.

> Your Husband & best friend for Ever & Ever.
> When I am gone, think of that, My Dear Emily & Children.
> W. M. Moxley

~

[*Emily Beck Moxley to William M. Moxley*]
Bullock, Ala.
Sept. 3, 1861
W. M. Moxley

Dear Husband,

It is now 8 or 9 oclock and I am siting by my table, trying to write to the object of my heart. For all the pleasure I see is in writing to you or reading a letter, and then I cant write nor read one from you with[out] crying, but it is a satisfaction to me if [I] do cry. I had rather write to you than to eat when I am hungry. The worst, I never know when to quit when I commence. That is not the case with you. Your letters are too short to suit me.

This leaves us all as common. My health is about the same that it was when I left you. Some days I feel very bad and others I feel very well. But do not let that trouble you, for I am not dangerous.[32]

Well, my Dear, I am home by my lone self to night except the children, and they are all a sleep and know not what trouble is. You cant imagine how I feel. It is so lonsome. If you could be with me to night, how diferent I would feel but that can not be. I have been at work on the door to night, trying to fix it so I could bar it up, and I got it fixt so I could fasten it. I have been proping it up untill I got tired of it, and I was afraid to lie down at night with the door open. That is the reason why I am so late to night, but I feel better in writing to [you] than any thing els. I can imploy my self at it if is at hour of midnight.

Well, Pa, I received you[r] kind letter last evening, which I was very

---

32. In September 1861, Emily Moxley was three months pregnant with her sixth child.

glad to get. I read it to the children and they all cried, and me with them. If you could have seen us you would have shed tears, too, I expect, but that you could not do. I wish you could have been here. Oh, what a time we do have. This evening Mat came down and set with me a while, and he read your letter and got to talking about you and Tom and Allen and we both took a cry again. He complains of your short letter to him.

Allen & Tom left Sunday morning. It nearly killed Allen to part with us all. He look like his heart would break. I wrote you all about that last Sunday. Pa sent for me on Friday evening and sent me home Sunday evening. Joe [Joseph J. Beck] come home with me and staid all night, but last night and to night is so lonely. You have no idea how bad the place looks with no person here but me and my little children.

Dear Husband, if I could but see you to night, oh, what would I give? Any thing in my reach, I would willing give for that kind favor, but that is out of my power to do. You told me to comb my hair ever time I thought of you. That is out of my power, for I would do nothing but comb it, for there is not one minute in the day but what I think of you. Ever where I go, there is where we have been together seting, walking, talking, standing, or lieing. There is allways something to bring you in my mind. There is your clothes, your old hat. They look so natural. There is two coats han[g]ing in my room that does look so much like the object that has worn them so much. Oh, how, how it does grieve me to [see] every thing that you have handled and thought so much of and things that you have made. But they all do you not good to night. Oh, I know you would be glad to come and set in this passage to morrow at noon and lie on the couch. I think of that so often. Dear Husband, this paper is wet with your wife's tears. They are shed for you, for one that I love more than heart can tell or words can express. It is the hardest trial I have ever had, by far. Dont you think it is hard for people to be seperated when they do think so much of each other? Oh, it is hard if it is fare. I know you will get tired of reading this letter, but I could write 8 pages and not get through. Then I could write all night and not get sleepy then.

I saw Parson Driskel[33] this evening. He came by here and told me some things, but not half enough. I got so full of cry that I could not ask any questions at all. The old man was the same way. I did want to

---

33. Allen Driskell is listed as a forty-nine-year-old preacher in the 1850 Coffee County census. He was married to a woman named Frances and had two children who would have been grown by 1861.

ask a good many questions, but did not. No one knows my troubles but my self. I try to conceal them as much as posible from every body. If I had a friend that I could talk to and tell my grief to, it would be a great saisfaction to me. But that friend I have not. I could talk to Ma and Sis, but they have enough to bear of their own. So I keep mine to my self and do the best I can, and that is bad. It seems to me that my only friend is gone, and it is nearly the case. I tell you, friends are scears in time of nead, but let a person be independent and they have friends on every hand. Them sort of friends are not worth haveing, but I hope some day I will not be beholding to any person, but I am now. I have no means of helping my self, but I put my trust in one that is able and willing to care of me if I will trust in him.

Well, you wanted to know how I was off for something to eat. I have had nothing since I came home but sidemeate and corn meal. That has been my condition untill now. Justice went to Elba[34] yesterday and he brought one fifty wieght sack of flour, and I now have a little dried beaf but the side of meate was very small and it is nearly gone, so my flour will do me no good unless I can get greece to go in it, and J[asper] has not sent for any thing for me yet. I do not know what I shall do yet. I do hate to go to any body and ask them to do for me unless I had the means for them to do with.

Oh, how I do miss my Dear William. If he was here all would be right, but as it is, I do not know how I shall come out. I am dependent. If I had of had the money you gave Justice, I could have sent by John Stinson[35] to M[on]tg[omery] after provision. He went up with the Pike Company, but I did not have one cts. Mary [Verlinda E. (Beck) Stinson] say we borrowed every thing they had to go upon before we left and eat it up. She told it in Pike and down here. She says we left them with out any thing. I told Mat about it. He hated it. I told him I would pay it if I done without my self, but he said for to wait untill I got more. I intend to pay her the flour, for I have it and can pay it if it takes it all.

I shall have to quit for want of room. You must receive all the love

34. Elba, originally Bentonville, was the seat of Coffee County.

35. John L. Stinson, fifty years old in 1860, was the father of John Lafayette Stinson and the father-in-law of Mary Verlinda E. (Beck) Stinson. He was also the father of Robert M. Stinson, who was married to Emily's cousin, Emiline, and of Micajah Jason Stinson, a sergeant in Company B, Twenty-fifth Alabama Infantry. A prosperous Pike County farmer, John Stinson owned twelve slaves in 1850. He died on 17 December 1864.

that pen and ink can put down from one that loves you dearly. So fare well for to night, my dear. When this you read, remember one that loves well though many miles apart we be, my love.

E. A. M. Moxley

Emily Moxley was visiting her husband
at Camp Johnston in October.

[*Jourdan Beck to William M. Moxley and Emily Beck Moxley*]
Alabama, Pike County
October 7th, 1861

Dear Son & Daughter,

Your letter came to hand last Friday. We were glad to hear from you & to hear you was all well. I feel sorry for you all that has to go to the north now it has got so late in the year. We are all as well as common except Joe. He has gone to bed with the headache. I dont know as there is any thing more the matter with him yet. He may be going to be sick. I got a letter from the boys [Charles A. Thompson Beck and Allen D. Beck] last Monday. They were all tolerably well. It rains & thunders like summer time.

I saw N[ewton Moxley] this morning. He was well. He has his hands full lately. There is rite smart of sickness about—more on the other side of the [Conecuh] river than in our settlement, though there is some near us. Mr. Hutchenson[36] got your horse & saddle & went on below.

I have nothing of importance to write We hear a good many rumors as usual without foundation. Lafayette[37] left here last Tuesday morning for Fort Gain[e]s.[38] He had mysed the chills two days.

36. Noah O. Hutchinson (22 February 1841–12 October 1913) of New Brockton, Alabama, was elected third sergeant on 15 November 1861 and later became Company A's fourth and final commanding officer. Pay and Muster Roll, Eighteenth Alabama Infantry, 31 December 1861, Alabama Department of Archives and History.

37. John Lafayette (Fate) Stinson, a Pike County farmer, was born on 5 November 1834. He was the son of John L. Stinson and was married to Emily's sister, Mary Verlinda E. Beck. He served as a private in Company B, Twenty-fifth Alabama.

38. Fort Gaines, on Dauphin Island at the mouth of Mobile Bay, was one of several installations constructed early in the nineteenth century to protect the port city of Mobile. The fortress, named in honor of Maj. Gen. Edmund Pendleton Gaines, was formally established in 1821, but

The river keeps so full we cant catch fish. I want to commence gathering corn as soon as the weather brakes off. I think I have one bale of cotton out. I want to have it gined & store it at home. I am a fraid I wont get enough for the second bale.

It is now 3 Oclock, & I want to go to the office, so I must close for the present. So, fare well for the present. All sends howdy to you all.

Yours as Ever,
Jourdan Beck

~

[*Emily Beck Moxley to William M. Moxley*]
Bullock, Ala.
Oct. 17, 1861
W. M. Moxley

Dear Husband,

I take my seat this evening to write you a few lines in hast[e], as I have a chance to send it by hand. I went down to the store and found a man over there that said he would take a letter to Garet Stanly[39] for me. We have no mail here now at all, only when any body will take it upon them selves to go after it. So you know it is a bad chance.

This leaves us all well as common. Davis[40] is some better than when I left you.

We all got a long very well untill we got to Greenville, then I was confused. I did not find any body there after me, so I hired a hack and

---

construction did not begin until 1853. Designed by chief engineer Joseph G. Totten as an irregular pentagon with twenty-two-foot-high walls of brick and sand, surrounded by a dry moat and armed with ten thirty-two-pounder cannon on each of the walls, plus four howitzers for each of the five bastions to defend against infantry assault, Gaines epitomized early nineteenth-century military architecture.

Alabama state troops occupied Fort Gaines, as well as Fort Powell and the stronger Fort Morgan, on 5 January 1861 and completed its construction in 1862. It remained in Rebel hands until August 1864. When the Pike Guards were mustered into Confederate service as Company B, Twenty-fifth Alabama Infantry, in Mobile in December 1861, the company was assigned to the garrison of Fort Gaines.

39. Garret Stanley was a thirty-one-year-old Coffee County farmer in 1860. After enlisting in the Bullock Guards he ran for the rank of fourth sergeant on 4 July 1861 but was defeated by Uriah Cory Curry by a vote of twenty-seven to eleven. He was in the hospital at Auburn on 31 December 1861 and was discharged the following month. He was married and the father of four small children.

40. Davis Moxley, William and Emily's youngest son, was one year old in 1861.

went to Mallet's hotell. Just as I got there I met W. Murrell. He was
on his way to Ft. Gain[e]s. He told me that there was a wagon on
behind after me. He said it would be in town that night. Newton got
John L. Williamson[41] to go after me so I got to New Providence Saturday night and to Pa's Sunday evening, and Pa sent me home Tuesday
morning, and that is my travels home.

Newton is hurt with Pa because he did not go after me and did not
like the way you done in doing every thing in such a hurry. He said
you did not give him time to do any, and he was very buisey at the
time and is yet. The reason Pa did not go after me is this: he had his
corn all pulled down and the pigs was destroying it and he had to hall
it out of the field. He said you struck him in the worst time you could.
I do not think Pa was as much to blame as Newton said he was, but
let that all pass now.

I had to pay half dollar for a hack in Greenville and one dollar and
a half at the hotell which left me 8 dollars, and then I gave Newton 3
dollars to get my provision home with. I could not make the change to
give him any less, so I have 5 dollars now.

Newton has fell out with Justice. Newton sent to him for some spirits, and Justice sent it to him and sent him word that he could not let
him have any more on credit, so that made Newton mad. Justice is
very sorry for it. He say he must sell for cash to get money to buy his
meat for next year. You dont [know] what hard times we have here.
There is very few in this country that has bacon.

Some body came in my house while I was gone and cut the lid of
your black trunk off. They could not get it unlockd, and they cut it off,
and they went in both rooms and the smoke house, but they did not
take any thing of much value. I miss some little things, but not much.

Dear Husband, I feel very lonesom since I came home. I am very
anxious to hear from you and to hear how you are, but I do not know
when I will hear from you as our mail is stop. The mail boy's mule
died. That is the reason why we have no mail. I hope he will soon get
another. Benjamin Singleton[42] has moved out of town and gone to his
mill.

I must close for the want of time, for the man is waiting over at the
store now. The children all send there love to you, and receive a good

41. John L. Williamson was a thirty-three-year-old carpenter in Pike County in 1860 and a
neighbor of Jourdan Beck.

42. Benjamin Singelton was a forty-five-year-old Coffee County farmer in 1860.

portion of love and respects to your self from your wife, one that wishes you well in this world and the world to come.

> So fare well for awhile, my dear W. M. Moxley.
> Emily A. M. Moxley and children
> W. M. Moxley
> at Auburn

~

[*Emily Beck Moxley to William M. Moxley*]
Bullock, Coffee Co,. Ala.
Oct. 20, [1861]
W. M. Moxley

Dear Husband,

I take my seat this sabbath night to write you a few lines to let you know that we are all tolerable well, and I hope this may find you a good deal better than when I last heard from you. I heard a letter read from J. Justice[43] Friday evening stating that you was very sick, which I was very sorry to hear, and I have been very uneasy ever since. I do wish I could be there to wait upon you. It would be a great satisfaction to me to be with you and wait upon you when you are sick. I was disappointed when I saw others reading letters from Auburn and there was none for me, but when I heard that you was sick I knew that you was very sick or you would have wrote me a few lines any how. I allso heard that you had lost your pocket book and all of your money, which I was very sorry to hear. If I had been there it would not have been the case, for you would have been at the house with me and I could have taken care of it for you. I left one week to[o] soon, and I do regret it so much. I do wish I had of staid longer, for I am so uneasy at this time I cant be satisfied any where nor in no condition. I am miserable and will be untill I hear from you again, which I hope to do soon for I have not received a line from you since I left you. Do let me hear from you

---

43. Joseph J. Justice, the son of Appelton H. Justice and Susan M. Justice, was twenty years old in 1860. He served first as second lieutenant and later as captain of Company A, Eighteenth Alabama Infantry, the third man to lead the Bullock Guards. He was killed in action at the battle of Chickamauga, 20 September 1863, and was placed on the Roll of Honor for gallant service on that field. He was replaced as captain of Company A by Noah O. Hutchinson. Wheeler, *Alabama,* 115–116.

soon. I sent a letter to Garret Stanly to take to you last Wednesday which I hope you have received.

It has been raining nearly ever [day] since I came home. It is lightning and thundering very heavy at this time and raining too, which makes me feell very lonsome and bad. I am afraid we will have bad wether before it fares off.

I must close for to night, and I will write more before I send it off. I do not know when that will be, for I shall send it by the first that goes to Auburn as there are two or three here from there.

Monday evening
Oct. 21, 1861

My Dear Husband,

I take my seat again this evening to write you a few more lines. This will inform you that I received your kind letter this morning which I was more than glad to get and was truly glad to hear that you was some better, but I am afraid that you was not much better for you was afraid that I would be uneasy and distressed which made you write as you did. Dear William, you dont know the uneasy hours I have spent since I heard that you was sick. I have not had a night sleep since, but all that I can do is to grieve. I go to bed but not to sleep much but to cry and study about my poor Husband that is lieing on his cot and no one to nurse him as I would do, or at least they would not do it as willingly as I would. Oh, what a pleasure it would be to me to be with you now. I never was so uneasy in my life as I am now. You dont know how I feel, for I think that you [would] lie and die before you let me know that you was sick.

But, my Dear Husband, you must be sure and let me hear from you as often as possible, but I fear when you leave Auburn that the chance for me to get a letter from [you] will be bad, for we have no mail here now and I dont know how long it will be before we get one started again. I dont know what I shall do then. I expect I would get a letter from New Providence sooner than any where els. I gess this will be the last letter that I will write to Auburn.[44] I shall have to wait untill you get to Huntsville and then write back before I will know where to

---

44. The Eighteenth Alabama, having completed its organization at Camp Johnson, had been ordered to Huntsville.

direct a letter to. I will send a letter to you to send to Ft. Gaines to Tom Beck. I will send the money to pay for it.

Well, I will tell you something about my corn. Charls McDay[45] has gathered it and put it in a house all together, and he dont want to pay [for] the corn, but I told him I must have it any how. He say his hogs have eat a good deal of it and he has used off of it ever since it would do to use, so you may know I will not get much. Mr. Wright[46] and Mr. [Appleton] Justice was here yesterday evening. Mr. Wright says he hope to geather the corn and he know how much was halled in, so I shall get him and Mr. Justice to attend to it for me. Newton has never been to see any thing about the corn nor any thing els, and every thing is just going to destruction as fast as it can.[47] Nobody to do any thing but me, and I cant do any thing by my self. You have lost all you had, and it looks like every thing here will be lost soon.

Newton dont want Justice to have any thing to do with your affairs, but he is the last friend I have got at this time, or at least appears to be, and I think he must be a friend or a great enemy one. He says C. Malloy has made him very mad about the corn and says he will take out an attachment and get it, any how, if I say so. I told him to do so. Newton wants to get all your notes and accounts and put them in the hands of an officer for collection. I dont know how that would suit you. I want your advise about it before it is done. Newton expects to go to your company in 3 or 4 weeks, but I dont think he will get off that soon, so I will close for this time and write some more before I send it off.

Tuesday Morning
Oct. 22, 1861

My Dear William,

I again take my seat to finish this letter, but it is with an aching heart that I do try to write and my tears falls so fast that I can hardly see to write for I am so troubled about you that I cant rest. When I am

---

45. Jackson McDay—who perhaps also went by the name Charles—was one of the Moxleys nearest neighbors.

46. William P. Wright is listed in the 1860 Coffee County census as a forty-six-year-old physician.

47. In 1890 his niece Mary Elizabeth (Moxley) Featherston reported that Daniel Newton Moxley "drinks a grate deal of his time"—a report corroborated the following year by Mary Verlinda E. Stinson—which might explain his apparent incompetence in helping to manage Emily Moxley's financial affairs.

a sleep I am dreaming about you. I dream last night of being with you and you was very sick and I thought we was geting some fruit but you was afraid to eat them. Some times I dream of seeing you in good health and in larges crowds of people and allso of being with you and giveing you money, but when I waked up I was by my self at home and on a good bed and my poor Husband in Camp Johnson being on his cot, and sick at that, and I cant be with him. But nothing in this world would give me more satisfaction than to be with you. If you dont get well soon I want you to send for me and let me be with you one time more. You must write to me again before you leave Auburn if you ever get able, and if you cant write get some body els to write for you, for I will be so anxious to hear from you.

There has been several deaths about here lately. Green Cody[48] has lost one of his sons and seveal others. Dr. Warren[49] attended to them. We are all well this morning but poor little Davis. He is not well yet. He has a hard time of it.

I must close for this time. You must write soon, Dear Husband. We all send our love to you and hope that this letter may find you better. Dear William, I must bid fare well, and I am afraid it will be a final adieu, so good bye my Dear.

Emily Moxley to my Dear Husband,
W. M. Moxley

48. Green W. Cody, a thirty-eight-year-old farmer from near Bullock, and his wife, Molly, had three sons in 1860: Michael, age eight; Southwood, age thirteen; and James, age fifteen. He was also one of the founders of the Friendship Baptist Church.

49. Sidney A. Warren was born in Wilkinson County, Georgia, in or about 1837, the son of Jesse Mason Warren and Mary (Breedlove) Warren. In 1860 he was a physician living with William and Emily Moxley, but within the year he married Martha E. Justice, the daughter of Appleton H. Justice and Susan M. Justice. The date of their marriage cannot now be determined, because Confederate deserters burned down the Coffee County courthouse on 3 September 1863. On 11 March 1862 Warren was elected second lieutenant of Company F, Thirty-third Alabama Infantry, commanded by his father-in-law. Sidney Warren's brother, William Henry Warren (born 17 October 1844), enlisted as a private in Company A, Eighteenth Alabama Infantry, in September 1863 and in 1903 was elected to represent Coffee County in the Alabama House of Representatives. Williams, *A Sketch of the 33rd Alabama Volunteer Infantry Regiment and Its Role in Cleburne's Elite Division of the Army of Tennessee, 1862–1865;* Owen, *History of Alabama,* 3:607–608.

2

"Good news as well as bad"

23 October 1861–22 November 1861

Recruiting and organizing eager volunteers proved easier than arming and equipping them. Tents, especially, proved hard to come by. Governor Moore predicted that lack of shelter for the recruits would "materially delay the encampment of the 3,000 troops," and he feared their becoming "to some extent demoralized" by confinement to camp while awaiting arms, equipment, and orders. "The sooner after acceptance that companies are mustered and go into actual service the better," he advised the secretary of war. Until the volunteers were actually on the march to the front, "there is great difficulty in keeping them."[1]

Accordingly, on 19 September 1861, the War Department assigned the yet raw Eighteenth, together with Col. Thomas James Judge's Fourteenth, Col. Thomas Hill Watts's Seventeenth, and Col. Joseph Wheeler's Nineteenth regiments of Alabama infantry to a new brigade to be commanded by Brig. Gen. Leroy Pope Walker. Walker, an Alabama native and a graduate of the University of Alabama, had been appointed the Confederacy's first secretary of war, but the welter of administrative detail and his inability to agree with Jefferson Davis on issues of states' rights prompted his resignation from the cabinet on 16 September 1861.

---

1. Andrew Barry Moore to Leroy Pope Walker, 21 July 1861, *OR*, ser. 4, vol. 1, p. 493.

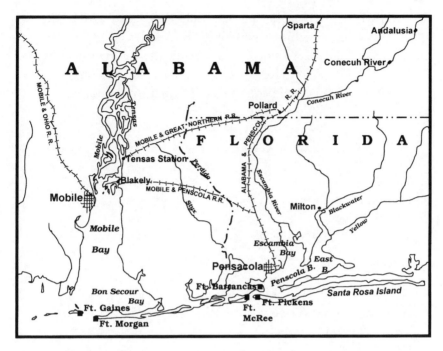

Figure 3. Mobile and Pensacola, 1862 (map by Susan Young)

The following day, 17 September, Davis commissioned him a brigadier general and ordered him to report with his still unarmed and un-
supplied brigade "as soon as it may be practicable" to Gen. Albert
Sydney Johnston at Memphis.[2]

But in the fall of 1862, disease was already beginning to stalk the
camps of the volunteers, killing a number of Captain Moxley's men and
leaving him dangerously ill for a number of weeks. With measles and
typhoid running rampant, Allen D. Beck reported to his sister Emily,
"We have one of the sarriest Doctors for our batalion you ever saw. He
cant tell the chill and fever from the head ache."

On the home front, in addition to her anxiety for her husband's
health, Emily Moxley was distraught to discover that the man who was
to have harvested her corn crop had appropriated it for his own and that

2. Judah P. Benjamin to Andrew B. Moore, 19 September 1861, *OR,* vol. 4, p. 416; Special Orders
Number 157, Adjutant and Inspector General's Office, Richmond, 19 September 1861, *OR,* vol. 52,
pt. 2, p. 152; Judah P. Benjamin to Leroy Pope Walker, Richmond, 19 September 1861, *OR,* vol. 52,
pt. 2, 192–193.

Newton Moxley, whom her husband had designated as his family's guardian, was evading his responsibility. "It looks like he is very tired of me and the children. A ready he is not willing to do any thing for me and them." With only twelve dollars to her name, she lamented that she had "not got George any pants yet" and feared that, with winter fast coming on, "the children may go bare footed."

[*Allen D. Beck to Emily Beck Moxley*]
Mrs. Emily A. Moxley
Bullock, Ala.
Politeness of R[obert] M. Stinson
Oct. 23rd, 1861
Head Quarters, Camp Loomis[3]

Dear Sister,

I take my pen in hand this evening to write you a few lines to let you know how we are getting along. We are getting along as well as usual. You ought to be here to see the skirmish drill, to see the big officers falling down on the ground and running through the woods. All the officers are talking about bringing their wives down here. Emily, you ought to come over and see us, and eat some of our good biscuits. We can cook as good as any body.

I expect you think hard of us for not writing to you before now, but you need not, for we did not know where you was. We cant hear from Auburn, and another thing was, we had no money to pay the postage and I thought it was scarse back there, so don't think hard of us. I think as much of you as I would if I had got a letter from you every week. I have not got but one letter from you all yet by mail. I have wrote three or four to Mat and have not received any one from him yet. Well, enough of that.

We are building houses here for winter quarters. If all the officers bring their wives here you must come to see us if we don't come home before Christmas. I think we will all be home by Christmas. R. M. Stinson & A. J. Capps[4] will start home to morrow if the boat comes,

3. Camp Loomis, near Mobile, was named for Col. John Q. Loomis of Coosa, Alabama, first commander of the Twenty-fifth Alabama Infantry. Loomis was wounded at Shiloh and at Murfreesboro and resigned from the army on 12 September 1862.

4. A near neighbor of the Becks, Andrew Jackson Capps was a twenty-seven-year-old farmer in 1860. He was elected sergeant of Company B, Twenty-fifth Alabama Infantry, but died of disease at Corinth, 27 April 1862.

which it will do if the wind is not blowing to[o] hard, and I want some of you to knit me a pair of wool gloves to ware when I stand guard these cold nights. I was on guard yesterday, and send them by Robert [M. Stinson].

All the officers are drilling now. We have one of the sarriest Doctors for our batalion you ever saw. He cant tell the chill and fever from the head ache. J. B. Stringer[5] & [Elias] Green [Stinson] are sick and have been for several weeks, and he pronounced it (their disease) different every morning, so you may know what sort of one he is.

I had better close, for I can't think of any thing worth writing. Tell the girls they must [not] marry before we get back. Give my love and respects to them all & receive a portion yourself so fare well for a while.

I remain your brother, as ever,
A. D. Beck

~

[*William M. Moxley to Emily Beck Moxley*]
Camp Johnson at Auburn
Oct. 25th, 1861
Mrs. E. A. M. Moxley

Dear Wife,

Your welcome letter came to hand yesterday. It was a balm to me, for I have spent an awful time since I have been confined to my tent. My cot became the most tiresome place I ever struck. I could not sleep but little after the noise of camp would cease. I would have a lonsome time untill day. You know I never could sleep when sick, even when I had you to watch over me. I dreamed of you evry night when I was sick. Some times when I would oppen my eyes I could hardly believe but you was some where not far from me. One time I a wake and found my arm extended as I had thought I had hold of your hand. Can you imagine the disappointment I met on waking, for when a sleep I was in you company and hold of your hand, that hand that has always been ready to afford me relief in sickness. But on waking I

5. John B. Stringer, the fifteen-year-old son of Wilson Baker Stringer and Margaret Ann (Williamson) Stringer, failed to return from his furlough and was reported as a deserter from Company B, Twenty-fifth Alabama Infantry, at Hall's Mill on 27 February 1862. Ironically, the Conscription Act passed by the Confederate Congress the following month mandated that all soldiers under the age of eighteen be released from duty.

found my self in tent on my cot and you in Coffee County, unconcious of my situation. I sufferd more with my hed than I ever did in my life. I was not clear of severe head ache for several days.

Last Sunday I went up [to visit] Conolye.[6] He came down the evening before & insisted I should go, but I was not able, but in the morning I went. It took my best to make the trip, but I did to my advantage, for I began to improve and to day I was able to walk to town for the first, though I had to walk slow.

My Dear Emily, [I] hope neither of us will be sick again unless we are prepared to wait on each other, for I never wanted to see you as much before. [If] every person in the world was present, it would [do] me no good if you was not, but I thank God I am mending as fast [as] I could expect, but I look worse than you ever saw me.

I have an other soldier I think will die, which [is] Ben Adams.[7] He had measels and was sent to Hospital & was doing well, I suppose, untill day before yesterday at dinner they gave him greens to eat that night. He was return worse yesterday morning. News reach me Ben was speachless, but I was not able to see that day, but I did go to day. I found [him] still speachless. I think he is bound to die, and if he does I shall send him home.

My dear Emily, I will now tell you, if I am able to travel, what time I will leave for Huntsville. It will be next Tuesday. 2 Companies will leave on Monday, but, as Maj. Holtzclaw has to go with the first, the Col. [Edward Bullock] did not want us to go togeather, as he wanted me to take charge of the division I went with, so I cant get off untill Tuesday.

Well, now I will say some thing about my money. 2 or 3 mornings ago one of the boys found my watch key that was in my purse 300 yards from my tent in a path. The rogue [k]new the key would detect him, so he throwed it a way. But I think I am on tract of him. One of the boys has been seen with money that did not have any nor never did. I hope in the morning I will be able to find out the rogue. It would help me, for the weather is cold and I want an over coat, an not one dollar to buy with.

I would write to the Esquire [Appleton H. Justice] if I could, but

6. This is perhaps Col. John F. Conoley of Dallas County, Alabama, commander of the Twenty-ninth Alabama Infantry, in which many of Moxley's old Barbour County friends were serving.

7. Pvt. Benjamin Adams died at Auburn, 28 August 1861. Pay and Muster Roll, Eighteenth Alabama Infantry, 31 December 1861, Alabama Department of Archives and History.

it will be late before I get yours done. Tell him to get that corn from Malloy if possible, & tell him to tell Charles Malloy [that] the reason he did not go to the war [was] that [he] wanted to stay & cheat the women & children out of what they had.[8] Tell Newton [Moxley] I do not want my papers put in suit unless when they are trying to thief from paying by fraudulent means. He has not written since you left there. I cant tell what is matter with him.

Well, I hope all things will work for our good. If our country can be set at liberty and I can get home to my family again, I think happiness will begin a new. I shall then expect to enjoy life, live happy, and die the same, but, my Emily, I can neither live happy nor die so where you are not. Kiss Willie Davis for me. Tell George, Betty, & Laura to be good that I may be well pleased with them when I get home & love them dearly.

Farwell, my Dear Wife & Children, for a while.
W. M. Moxley

(NB) We had a fight In Virginia which resulted in the defeat of the Yankies well. Killed 1000 took 600 prisoners cap[tive]. On our side, killed & wounded, 300. This took place last Monday.[9]

W. M. Moxley

~

[*William M. Moxley to Emily Beck Moxley*]
Oct. 26th, 1861

My Dear Emily,

I am still improving this morning. I wish I could see you an the children at this time & know how you all are. Ben Adams is still alive,

8. Charles Malloy did ultimately join the army, serving as a private in Appleton Justice's Company F, Thirty-third Alabama Infantry, until his death at St. Mary's Hospital in Dalton, Georgia, sometime before 6 May 1863.

9. On 21 October 1861, Brig. Gen. Nathan G. Evans's Confederate brigade caught 1,700 Union troops under Col. Edward D. Baker attempting to cross the Potomac River near Leesburg, Virginia. On the steep and wooded south bank, locally known as Ball's Bluff, the Rebels severely mauled the brigade, killing Baker and 49 of his men and wounding 158 more. An additional 714 were reported missing as the routed Federals attempted to regain the north bank of the river. Evans reported 36 killed, 117 wounded, and 2 missing. Although trifling by later standards, the engagement at Ball's Bluff had a profound effect on both Northern and Southern morale.

but I think he will soon die. Capt. Brady[10] sent one of his men home this morning, a corpse.

I have found my purse, but the rogue had spent all but 30 dollars. But I think I shall get it out of his wages. It was Bill Kelly that stold it, but he had help to spend it.

Oh, Emily, I want to see you so bad. There is no happiness for me without you, my dear. Please quit the use of snuff for my sake.[11] I have quit the use of tobacco & dont expect to use any more untill I see you again. I cant tell how long that will be untill I get to Huntsville. Then I will let you know. Tell Mat to write to me, as he has not answered my last. Give him my best wishes. Tell him I want to see him very bad. If he was hear, I would play a game of Drafts with him.

So fare well, Dear Emily
W. M. Moxley

~

[*William M. Moxley to Emily Beck Moxley*]
Camp Johnson
Oct. 26/61
E. A. M. Moxley

Dear Wife,

Knowing how anxious you are to hear from me, I have concluded to write you again, [and] as I started a letter to you this morning, but knowing that I shall have an opportunity of sending this sooner, or so as to reach you sooner than the other, for your satisfaction I write again, though I can write nothing but what I have written, which you

10. James T. Brady was the first captain of the "Covington Hunters," Company B of the Eighteenth Alabama. He resigned from the service on 24 February 1862 and was replaced by S. D. McLelen.

11. The use of snuff by Southern women of the "poor white" and yeoman classes was not at all uncommon. Lt.-Col. Arthur James Lyon Fremantle of Her Majesty's Coldstream Guards, touring the Confederacy in 1862, recorded in his diary that "Texan females are in the habit of dipping snuff—which means putting into their mouths instead of their noses. They rub it against their teeth with a blunted stick" (Lord, *The Fremantle Diary*, 37). One might recall the Widow Douglas in *Huckleberry Finn*, a most respectable woman. "She took snuff, too," Huck informs his reader; "of course that was all right, because she done it herself" (Mark Twain, *Adventures of Huckleberry Finn*, facs. ed. [New York: Oxford University Press, 1996], 19).

will get soon. It will be sent to Thomas Wasden's.[12] The reason I can send this to you [is that] Ben Adams is dieing, and I shall send him home. You will see in the other letter all the history of his case and my own. I can say in this, I have been very sick and I never wanted to see my Emily as bad in my life. I tell you, I wanted some of that nursing I always received from your willing hands. But, thank God, I am mending as fast as I could expect, but I had a bad time for 5 or 6 days which made me think of home many times. But you will hear my story when you see the other.

I have some good news as well as bad. I fortunately got on tract of my money several days ago. This morning I [recovered] it, or a portion of it. I only got 30 dollars, but I will get it all, for I will save it out of his wages. It was Bill Kelly that took [it]. He gave 60 dollars of it to one of Capt. Brady's men to keep for him and spent 30 dollars, & Kelly spent the balance. So I cant reach [it] yet a while. I tell you, it releaved me when I found where it was. Think of my condition when sick, & bad sick at that. In my tent, on my cot, without a dollar nor no person to cheer me—nothing but the common noise of the camp. Some grunting [?], some playing cards, some fiddling, some dancing, others enjoying them selves as they saw fit, regardless of evry thing but themselves.

You must not think hard of this letter, for I sit up last night and wrote you a long letter. I wrote to you my company would not leave untill next Tuesday. When you get it, you will know the reason. When we get to Huntsville, I will find out how long we are expected stay, &, if long, I will send for you at wonce. But I cant tell how it will be yet. One thing I know: that is, I shall never be happy sepperated from evry thing on earth that is near & dear to me. I want you to write to me by who ever goes to Coffee.

I received a blanket this morning, but I dont know who sent it. I expected you would send me a blanket, but I see this is niether of your blankets. Well, you can let me know all about it.

I must close. Be sure to write as soon and as often as you can, and I will do the same, for your letters give me more happiness than evry thing else. So write often, for when I am writing I have you present in my imagination all the time.

We had a big fight last Monday in Virginia. We whiped the Yankies

12. Thomas Wasden, in 1860, was a twenty-nine-year-old Bullock merchant, owning a store not far from the Moxley home.

badly. Killed 1000, took 600 prisoners. They killed and wounded 300 of our men.

Farwell, Dear Emily & Children, for awhile.

~

[*Emily Beck Moxley to William M. Moxley*]
Bullock, Coff[ee] Co., Ala.,
Oct. 28[, 1861]
W. M. Moxley

Dear Husband,

I take my seat this Monday night to write you a few lines to let you know how we are. This leaves us tolerable well, and I hope it my find [you] the same. I got a letter from you this evening which I was very glad to get, and more than all to hear that you was getting well and that you had got on track of your money. I know you did feel very bad when you was sick and your money all gone. You dont know how I felt about you. I have seen no satisfaction since I left you, but I feel a great deal better to night than I have felt before, becaus I think you are better than you have been, and do sincerely hope you continue to mend.

Well, my Dear Husband, you said you got a blanket but you did not know who sent it and said it was not one of mine. I gess it is, for I started one of them to you last Thursday by [Noah O.] Hutchinson. It was in the satchel that you borrowed for me when I left Auburn. I never thought to mention it in the letter that I sent you. The letter was sent by Colquitt.[13]

Write. I think I have not got the letter that you sent by T. Wasden yet. I would be glad to see it.

I got a letter from Allen yesterday. He says they have some sickness there. He says that John [B.] Stringer and [Elias] Green Stinson is very sick. They are a going to send them home soon.[14] They have been sick a long time. He says they have a very sorry Dr. there.

Robbert Stinson is at home at this time. He has come home to[o] soon. Emiline is not down yet. That is bad.[15]

13. This is perhaps Alfred Colquett, a Bullock merchant.

14. Elias Green Stinson died 2 April 1862 at Corinth, Mississippi. He was only one of five Stinsons in Company B, Twenty-fifth Alabama, to die of disease or wounds between December 1861 and September 1863.

15. Emiline E., the wife of Robert M. Stinson, was about nine months pregnant at this time. Her husband had taken leave to be at home with her for the birth of their first child.

Allen says he cant hear from Auburn at all. I dont think that you directed your letters right. You will have to direct them to Ft. Gain[e]s by the way of Mobiele. He says that Mobiele is the nearest [post] office [and] that there is no office at Ft. Gain[e]s. When you write again, direct your letters to Ft. Gain[e]s by way of Mobiele in care of Capt. Curtice, commanding Pike Gards.[16] That is the way they back the letters here, and [they] go right.

Ma and Sis was down here last week. They come Thursday evening and staid untill Saturday morning. Newton come a Thursday too. He staid untill Friday evening. He went to see C. Maloy about that corn. He says he will do what is right. He complaines of me and you being so careless about every thing, and I do the very best I can do, but I cant please him. I told him the other day that he was as careless as either of us. It looks like he is very tired of me and the children. A ready he is not willing to do any thing for me and them. He dont want me to have any thing to do with Justice or any of his people, and I dont know what I would do if it was not for Justice.

He is the only friend that I have found that proves to be a friend in need, and he is. If I want a horse, he told me I could get one, and if I need any thing that he has, I can get it. So what more could I ask? And then Newton dont want me to borrow any thing, not go about his store, and what would I do if I wanted to send to Mill? Send all over the neighborhood to borrow a horse and then not get one? They have proved true friends to me.

I have got my provisions at home at last. They come Saturday. I sent by [Dr.] W. [P.] Wright after them. They cost me 2.$ 75 cts. to get them home. The freight was one dollars and a half to Greenville, and then I paid W. Wright one dollar 25 cts. for halling them home. They have cost me 5 dollars and 75 cts. I gave Newton 3 dollars to have them brought to me, but he did not do it, so I had to see to it my self. I have no idea of ever seeing the money any more, and the children may go bare footed. I have but 12 dollars now. I had to pay 2 in Greenville and 5.75 for my provision, with that Newton has. So you see how I am treated. I have not got George any pants yet, either, nor cant get them without the money. I think Newton ought to have give me back the money. I told him I had sent for the things and I told him that you

16. John B. Curtis of Pike County was the first captain of the Pike Guards, or the Pike County Volunteers, Company B, Twenty-fifth Alabama Infantry. He resigned from service on 15 January 1862 and was succeeded by Napoleon B. Rouse, who was in turn replaced by Daniel Newton Moxley, the brother of William M. Moxley.

gave me that money to get the children some shoes with. Enough of that now.

If I could see you I could tell you a heap that has happend. Mat's negro woman has a fine white baby and she say D. N[ewton Moxley] is the father of it.

You must excus bad writing this time, my Dear William, for I had to write down before the fire with the paper on my lap. The children are all asleep and I am alone. My Dear, you must write soon and often, for I am so glad to get a letter from you, for you are the only friend that I have, my dearest deare.

So fare well, my Dear Husband, for this time yours untill death. Emily A. Moxley

Dear Husband, we are all well this morning. I would send you a bed quilt by Wasden if he could take it to Greenville. I have not seen him yet, but I hope I may see him this morning.

I must close. Oh, if I could see my Dear it would be more satisfaction to me than any thing els in the world, but I can not.

> So farewell, my Dear Husband, for a while.
> Emily A. Moxley
> to W. M. Moxley

From the beginning of the secession crisis, Fort Pickens, located on Santa Rosa Island in Pensacola Harbor, had been a major flash point, and when Florida seceded on 10 January 1861, the Federal garrison in and around Pensacola, Florida, withdrew within its walls, beyond the range of Rebel guns. The Davis administration, therefore, sent Brig. Gen. Braxton Bragg to Pensacola to take command of the Confederate forces besieging the fort. By mid-April 1861, Union reinforcements had made the fort invulnerable to Confederate attack, and blockading Federal warships rendered the port useless to the South.

Following the loss of Forts Henry and Donelson, Bragg was ordered to evacuate the Rebel garrisons from the Alabama and Florida coast and move them to Corinth, Mississippi, where Albert Sidney Johnston was concentrating troops for a Confederate counteroffensive. On 27 February 1862, Bragg wrote to Brig. Gen. Samuel Jones, the Confederate commandant at Pensacola, that in "the great strait to which we are re-

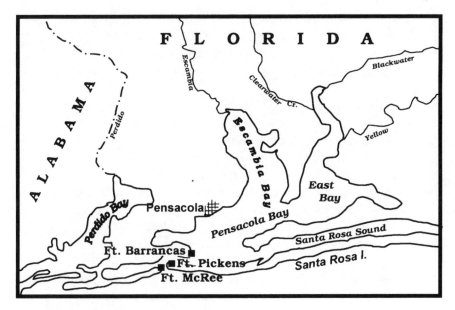

Figure 4. Pensacola, 1862 (map by Susan Young)

duced it has become necessary to concentrate our resources even at the cost of giving up some of our important positions." He instructed Jones, therefore, to "make all dispositions at the earliest moment, working day and night, to abandon Pensacola." The last Confederate troops evacuated Pensacola on 9 May 1862, and Federal forces occupied the city the following day.[17]

[*Two letters enclosed, one from each of the two Beck brothers*]

[*Allen D. Beck to Emily Beck Moxley*]
Fort Gaines, Ala.
Nov. 5th, 1861

Dear Sister,

I take my pen in hand this morning for the purpose of letting you know how we are getting along. We are as well as common. I am sorter puney but not sick. I cant make a strait line this morning. We

17. *OR*, vol. 6, p. 835.

moved back to the Fort last week. There is some talk of us going to
Pensacola, but I am afraid it is not true. I had rather go to Pensacola
than to stay here. If we should go down there, I would be glad if you
all could meet us in Greenville, for we will go by there, I expect, if we
go atall.

The measeals are in camps here.[18] There was three or four deaths
here last week. There were two burried in one day. There is one of our
men in the hospital that will die before morning, I expect. The Dr. say
there is no chance for him. His name is Killpattric.[19] John [Stringer] &
Green [Stinson] are mending, but they mend slow.

We received your letter the other day and was very glad to hear
from you. I cant write this morning, so I will quit and let Tom write.

You said something about needing cloth[e]s. I will need some pants,
but I expect I can get them cheaper here than you can back there, or as
cheap any how.

J. M. Stringer[20] sends his best respects to you. I will close. Recieve
my best & respects, also give my love to all my relatives.

> I remain your brother, as ever,
> A. D. Beck

We look for Bob S[tinson] to day. I hope we will get some news
from him. We are all as glad to see some person from home as if he
was a brother.

[The second letter written on reverse of letter above]

---

18. Due to its prevalence and to the many complications such as pneumonia and mastoiditis that often accompanied it, measles was perhaps the most dreaded of the so-called eruptive fevers. It followed only diarrhea, dysentery, and "inflammation of the lungs" as the leading cause of death among Confederate captives in Northern prison camps. Brooks, *Civil War Medicine*, 120, 126. Valuable information on disease in the Confederate army may be found in Hallock, "Lethal and Debilitating"; Cunningham, *Doctors in Gray;* and Steiner, *Disease in the Civil War.*

19. This is apparently Joseph Killpatrick, fifth sergeant of Company E, Twenty-fifth Alabama Infantry. John Killpatrick, of the same company, was wounded at Murfreesboro. Company E was recruited in Pickens County.

20. James M. Stringer, the son of Wilson B. Stringer and Margaret Ann (Williamson) Stringer, was listed as a twenty-one-year-old medical student on the Pike County census of 1860. He was elected second lieutenant of Company B, Twenty-fifth Alabama Infantry, when the regiment was organized at Mobile in December 1861 but resigned from the service on 22 June 1863.

[*Charles A. Thompson Beck to Emily Beck Moxley*]
Fort Gain[e]s, Ala.

Dear Sister,

I will write you a few lines this morning my self, but I feel some what dull from being on gard last night. The boys are all in fine spirets this morning and ingoying them selves very well. We draw syrip, potatoes, and pickle pork. We fare verry well in the eating line. Our company enjoyes very good health. We have some few deaths heare, but it is not caused from the unhealthyness. It is as healthy a place as there is in the Sothern Confederacy.

We have no news heare of importance. We can not write you any news for that reason. You expect to heare all the news when you get a letter, I know, but you do not get it. You must write me all the news when you writ all about the girls. That is the most interesting of any thing you can wrte. You must tell Miss Caty, Liddy, Nancy, and Sislyann howdy for me, and all the rest you can see, and tell them to remember me. I think of them often.

Well, good morning, George.[21] Dont you wish you were heare to help me eat oysters and fish. We have aplenty of them heare. You must come to the ware and learn to shoot yankees, though I am afraid we will never have to shoot them heare.

Come hear Bill,[22] and heare Uncle Tom. He sends howdy to Billy and the baby, to also to Betty and Larra.[23] You all must be good children and learn to write so you can write to me a letter. I would be glad to git a letter from you.

I have nothing of importance to write, so I must close. Emily, you must write often. I will never forget you. I would have written to you sooner, but I knew not where to direct a letter. I [had] not a cent to pay postige. You must excuse me for not paying postige. Tell Mat to write often. He can interrest me the most of any other one that has written to me. My happyest moments is when I am reading letters

21. George Edwin Moxley, the eldest son of William and Emily Moxley, was nine years old at the date of this letter.

22. Bill is William and Emily's three-year-old son, William Jasper Moxley.

23. These are William and Emily Moxley's daughters, Mary Elizabeth, born in 1855, and Laura, born in 1856.

from my Deare brothers, sisters, & parrents. Write me the latist news from the Dr. when you write.[24] He never writes to me.

> C. A. T. Beck
> High Private of the First Ala. Batalion[25]
> I remain your affectionate brother as ever,
> C. A. T. B.

~

[*D. Newton Moxley to William M. Moxley*]
New Providence, Ala.
Nov. 9th/1861
Capt. Wm. M. Moxley

Dear Brother,

After a long delay, I again resom my seat to write you a few lines as I have not heard from you in somtime. Sopose that you are well a ware of the reason of my delay, tho you may think that I have had the oppertunity of writing before this, all so. I might of written som time, but when I could of written it was not mail day, & you have som idey how [a doctor?] feeales when he is going both night & day.

I have booked 542.00 dollars in the month of Oct. & 700.00 since I seen you in Greenville, so you can have som [k]nolage of the sickness that has bin in the country.

I was at Bullock last week, and all your famaly were in fine health. I went to see sumpthing about that corn. Malloy had githered it all & put it to one crib, & I soposed that he said that you should not have enny of it, but when I went to see him he said that you might have the corn & that [*word illegible*] help him gather it & haul all of it & that [William P.] Wright would haul your part to you.

I saw som of your friends, & they expressed great anxiety to hear from you.

The health of the people is getting better at this time. I regret

---

24. The Beck family often refers to William Moxley as "the Doctor," or "Dr.," as he was a physician in civilian life.

25. The First (Loomis's) Alabama Infantry Battalion was consolidated with the Sixth (McClellan's) Infantry Battalion to form the Twenty-fifth Alabama Infantry Regiment.

mutch to hear of your bad health & misfortune. I have bin fearful of such an axident to you.

Now I want to ask your advise about my leaving home. You have bin in the army long enuff to tell sumpthing about it, whether the goverment will be able to pay the expensis or not. So you see that if it was to fail, it would be a bad business for me, for it is making a grait sacrifice, but I want to do the best I can for ous bouth and country. You have no idey how times has changed since you left hear. Thar is no money to be had in all this country, not nothing to be had with out the money. The people are hauling corn to Greenville to sell for salt & c. No man expects to pay one dolar this year, so you have some idey how this country is getting on. So I want you [to] give me your opinion as to what you think I had better com to the army or stay hear. If thar is no [*word illegible*] in the goverment, I think it would be the best for me to com, for money is going to be [*word illegible*] at best, and I want you [to] writ to me what I shall need & all the arangments that you want me to make.

I shall have to git som clothing maide before I com, and I shall have to sell my stock to git som money to com on. Writ me how mutch it will tak[e] & c. If you can throu the goverment make som arangment for my transportation, I would be glad for you to do so, and if thar is enny medicine that I have got that I will need, writ to me, for I am perfectly willing to do what is the best for ous.[26]

So I want you to writ as soon as you get this, for I want to git ower business all in notes before I leave, & if I com I shall have G. W. Williamson[27] to attend to mine.

I was talking to Emaly about yours, and she said that you thout that Justice would be a good hand. He would, provided he had no liens[?] of his o[w]n on the people, but you [k]now that he would colect for him self first, & yours would be for the last.

The people seams to regret my leaving very mutch, bouth in your country & in this. They say that they will be left without enny doctor.

I must come to a close for the want of time. I want you to write

26. Daniel Newton Moxley joined, and eventually became captain of, Company B, Twenty-fifth Alabama Infantry.

27. Green W. Williamson was a forty-three-year-old merchant from the Haw Ridge region of Coffee County.

soon as you get this, & if it will not hit the mail hear, direct your letter
to Greenville.

Yours respectfully
D. N. Moxley

~

[*William M. Moxley to Emily Beck Moxley*]
Huntsville, Ala.
Nov. 12th, 1861
E. A. M. Moxley

Dear Wife,

I again write to from this place to keep you from being uneasy
about [me,] for I know if you hear that I was left at Huntsville & Regiment gone to Mobile[28] you would at wonce think I was Dangerous,
but I hope this will reach you before you hear it from any other source.

Well, my Dear Emily, you never saw me sick as I have been the day
I wrote to you. I was taken down & compleetly prostrated on Wednesday. I was brought to [the] place I am now at, one of the best places in
the world, the same day the Reg. was ordered to Mobile. That night
[N.] Jasper [Moxley] started home. Now think of my condition. 500
miles from home, my company about to leave me 400 mile, and left a
mong strangers & not knowing wheather I should live or die.

Well, now, I will say something about my sickness. Well, when I
found out I had got into a dangerous condition, I sent to town &
bought some med[icine] & took it. The family waited on me as well
as it could been done on earth except [by] you. They have over 100
Negroes. Well, I lay here 3 days, the sickest soul you ever saw, shacking
almost continually as bad as you ever saw me. Dont you know I suffered. But, thank God, my Fever is gone. I have not had any in 3 days.
My strength is all I want now to put me on foot again.

I cant, for the want of strength, write half as much as I want to. I
expect to start for Mobile next Sunday, then I will write you again. I
was up early this morning, washed my face & hands, & sat up & eat
my Breakfast. 2 time I have got out of bed to eat since came here.

My Dear Wife, I must close for want of strength. My pen in my

28. Soon after the Eighteenth Alabama was posted to Huntsville, its orders were changed and it
was transferred to the defenses of Mobile. Bergeron, *Confederate Mobile.*

hand [is] unsteady. Dont be uneasy, for if you believe, you see I have missed the Fever 3 days with care. I will soon be well, but I could not get well in Camps.

Tell all the children Pa wants to see them bad. I thought of them often while I was so low.

Your Effectionate Husband,
W. M. Moxley

~

[*Emily Beck Moxley to William M. Moxley*]
Bullock, Ala.
Nov. 14, 1861
W. M. Moxley

Dear Husband,

I take my seat this Thursday night to write you a few lines to let you know howe we are. This leaves some of us not very well. I am not well my self, but I feel a good deal better to night than I did last night. I was right sick yesterday, and poor little Davis is not well. He is worse to day than common with his bowels. The rest is well.

This will inform you that I received your kind letter to night and hasten to answer it as Mr. Justice is a going to go to Elba to morrow. You do not know how proud I was to get your letter, for I had got very uneasy about you, but I hope you will still mend.

I am afraid you will not get this, for I heard last night that you were in Mobille or that Bullock's regiment was there. Capt. Curtice, J. L. Stinson, Jasen Stinson, [Elias] Green Stinson, [and] John Stringer [29] is come home very sick. I have not seen them, but Mat was here last night. He saw Fate, and he told Mat that Bullock's regiment and Love's [30] regiment was ordered to Ft. Gaines, and they had all ready got

29. Micajah Jason Stinson was the son of John and Martha C. Stinson and was listed as twenty years old on the 1860 Pike County census. Elected sergeant of Company B, Twenty-fifth Alabama Infantry, he was wounded at Chickamauga, 20 September 1863, and died sometime before 2 May 1864.

30. This is most likely Col. Zachariah Cantey Deas's Twenty-second Alabama Infantry, which was, in fact ordered to the defense of Mobile in the winter of 1861. Andrew P. Love of Pike County was the captain of Company I. Love was wounded at Shiloh and was forced to resign from the army on 1 July 1862. Upon recovery, however, he became commanding officer of the Fourth Alabama (Love's) Cavalry Battalion, three mounted companies recruited between August and September

to Mobille. He said they got there a day or two before he left, and he left Ft. Gaines Monday morning and got to Pa's Tuesday night. I hope it is so, but I fear it is not.

Dear Husband, you have no idea what a miserable time I have spent since I left my Dear William. The time appears long to me to be parted from the Dearest object on earth to me, my all, for when you are gone from me I am one to my self, no one to talk to as I would like to. I have no one to come to see me, and I hardly ever go any where. I stay at home and grieve and mourn for one that is far from me, for one that is deare to me: that is my Dear Husband. Oh, but I could be with him to night, how happy I would be, but that is imposible at this time.

You said I could go to Huntsville from Greenville in two days if I could stand it, day and night. I would stand any[thing] to get to my Dear Husband if it was in my power to do so. You said you would send me the money to go with in two weeks. I do not know yet what arrangement I can make with the children, but I am sirtain that Pa will take Betty and George, but I dont think they would be willing to take Laura and Willie. I shall have to take them with me. I gess it will not cost much to pay there way, but I will try them and see what they will do.

I was up there last week. Mat took me and the children up there in the ox waggon a Thursday morning, and Pa sent me home Sunday evening and had me some wood and lightwood hauled a Monday.

Pa says you have not wrote to him in a long time. He think you ought to write to him oftener than you do. He says he is glad to hear from you often.

My Dear Husband, if you send me money to go to Huntsville, I will go if I can, if I have to take Laura and Willie with me, that is if there is enough of it to pay our expenses there. Then, if you are not there, what will I do? You must give me instructions how and what to do in your next letter and be sure to send me money enoughf, for if there is to[o] much you can have it back, for I have not got one cts.

I give the last cent I had for some cloth to make George some pant which I could not get without no money. Newton kept three dollars of

---

1863 in Barbour and Pike Counties. Ordered to Virginia, Love's battalion took part in the fighting at the Wilderness, Spotsylvania Court House, North Anna, Cold Harbor, Trevilian Station, and the siege of Petersburg. Captain Love was captured at Dinwiddie Courthouse, 31 March 1865. Wheeler, *Alabama*, 301.

the money you give me, and I shall have to borrow money to pay the postage on this letter. I have done the best I could with it. If I was to start and not have money enoughf, I dont know what I would do.

You must do as you please and as you think best, but I want to be with you very bad. I dream of you every night. I think you come home. I dreamed two [or] three times that you had come home and I was so happy with you. I thought you sent me your picture. I thought you had it taken and was seting writing when it was taken. I thought it did look so natuaral and so good, and I was so glad to get it, but when I awoke I found it not so. Oh, but it was true.

My Dear Husband, you know my condition. My time will be out the last of Febuary. Emiline has a fine boy. It was borned Teusday night. She had Newton [Moxley] with her [as attending physician]. I have not seen him but one since I come home. I dont know what he is a going to do.

Well, my Dear Husband, I must close, for my eyes hurte me and I cannot write any more. When this you read, remember your wife in old Coffee, but would not be there if she could get away, for I had rather be any where els than here. It is so lonesome and so desalate. You must write as soon as you get this, and write more the next time, for it is so much pleasure to me to read a long letter from my Dear. I nearly get them by heart reading them over so often.

> So fare well, my Dear, for this time.
> Emily A. M. Moxley

~

[*N. Jasper Moxley to William M. Moxley*]
Jefferson Co., Georgia
Nov. 14, 1861

Dear Brother,

I take my seat to write you a few lines which I hope will find you in better health than you were in when I left you. I am now at Cousin Martha Cheatham's. I got hear last Friday. I was very sick when I got hear, but I am men[d]ing very fast. I think I shal[l] be well in a few days.

Thear is a great [d]eal of sickness in this settlement, and several deaths since I saw you. Mrs. Noah Smith, she dyed with dropsy at the heart,[31] and a young man by the name of John Summers, he dyed with Newmonia. Rufus Weeks is now very low with Typoid fever. The scarlot fever is in the settlement. George Farmer has lost two of his Daughters and a negro girl.

Cousin Martha's family are all well except John. He has bin very sick all day. My family are all well except colds. You must write to me soon as you get this, for I am very uneasy about you.

I expect to start to Frank Parker's in the morning. The Batty Guards[32] are all come back and are going on the coast. I wish your company could be so fortunate as to be sent back too.

The women & children [are] coming in to Augusta from Savanah. They are expecting an atact at Savanah soon.[33] They are sending of[f] al[l] their salt & specia.[34] They think several men has left, drest in

---

31. "Dropsy" or more properly "hydropsy" of the heart is now known as hydropericardium, oedema, or congestive heart failure. The disease is characterized by retention of fluid around the heart and is treated with digitalis, a preparation of foxglove leaves.

32. The unit called Battey Guards was raised in Jefferson County, Georgia, 1 October 1861. It was named for its first captain, William H. Battey, who was killed at the battle of Sharpsburg, 17 September 1862. When mustered into Confederate service at Decatur the unit became Company G of the Thirty-eighth Georgia Infantry, also known as Wright's Georgia Legion. From November 1861, through June 1862, the Thirty-eighth Georgia was assigned to the Department of South Carolina, Georgia, and Florida and saw duty at Skidway Island and Savannah but was then transferred to the Army of Northern Virginia, with which it served until the surrender at Appomattox. Henderson, *Roster of the Confederate Soldiers of Georgia*, 4:177; Sifkas, *Compendium of the Confederate Armies*, 248.

33. As early as 28 May 1861, the U.S. Navy instigated a blockade of Savannah's harbor, but not until 4 November 1861 was the port city threatened with capture when Brig. Gen. Thomas W. Sherman and Flag Officer Samuel F. DuPont sailed into Port Royal, north of Savannah, with a force of 77 war ships and 12,000 troops. Three days later, on 7 November, DuPont's fleet pounded Forts Beauregard and Walker on Hilton Head into submission, and Sherman's infantry quickly landed to occupy the island. The following day, Robert E. Lee arrived in Savannah to take charge of the defense of the Department of South Carolina, Georgia, and East Florida. Nevertheless, on 24 November, Sherman's forces landed on Tybee Island, Georgia, on the Savannah River, thus blockading the vital harbor and moving within striking distance of Fort Pulaski, the city's main defense. Its guns silenced and its wall breached in two places by thousands of rounds from Federal heavy artillery, the brick fort surrendered on 11 April 1862. Not until 21 December 1864, however, did the city itself fall, when William T. Sherman culminated his march to the sea by entering Savannah and offering it as a "Christmas gift" to Abraham Lincoln.

34. Heeding the call of the *Charleston Mercury* to "let the torch be applied whenever the polluter invades our soil," on 29 November 1861, Georgia and South Carolina planters burned thousands of bales of cotton rather than allow them to fall into Union hands.

female clothing, and come to Augusta. The Batty G[u]ards has to pick up all the double barrel guns & rifles they can get & start Sunday morning for Savanna.

I want you to write to me the name of the medicine you told me to get to make pills, for I have forgot what it was. I must come to a close. Be shure to write soon. Molley sends her love to you and Thomas. Give my best regards to Thomas, acquaintences, and also to your self

from your true brother,
N. J. Moxley

[*Sarah E. Moxley Brooks to William M. Moxley*]
[14 November 1861]
Thursday night

Dear Brother William,

I have neglected to write to you all this time. I will try to write you a few lines which I hope will find you in good health, but I fear your health will not be good soon, for you have to be exposed so much in camp. I hope you will take good care of your self. I have bin very uneasy about you ever since Jasper came home and told me how you were. I hope you will forgive me for not writeing to you, for I have thought a hundred times that I would write, but neglected it.

I have no news to write to you that would be entertaining. My health is tolerable good at this [time]. The people are dying up very fast. Tell Thomas about John Simmons being dead, [and] tell him that I was very sorry that he never come to see me before he left. Tell him to write to me how he is satisfied since he joined the company.

William, please write to me & address your letter to Hopefull & Burke Co., in the care of John D. Cook. Talk to Thomas and tell him to do better & not gamble & do wickedly, for he dont know what time he may have to die.

Write to me what your [post] office is & how I can direct letters to you.

I must close. My best love to you & Thomas.
Sarah E. Brooks

~

[William M. Moxley to Emily Beck Moxley]
Huntsville, Ala.
November 15th, 1861
E. A. M. Moxley

Dear Wife,

Though I wrote to you so recently, I feel this morning that I cant spend my lonely hours more satisfactory to myself than writing to you, for it is the next thing to conversing, which would give me a great [d]eal of pleasure.

Well now, something about my health. Yesterday was the 9th day since I was deposited in this room and yesterday was the first time I left it in 9 days. I went below in the morning [*illegible phrase*] in the Old Ladies Room. She is a good hand to talk and appears to be a very pious Methodist. She conversed freely on Religious subjects. She was good company for me. Any way, her Daughter came, one that has not been married long. She did wish you could be here with me. She said it would be so much more satisfaction for us to be togeather, but I know she could not imagine how much happiness it would give me.

Well, I past of[f] yesterday much better than any previous day since I came here. I walked about 50 yds in the evning and back this Morning. I felt still stronger. I dressed myself and went down to Breakfast for the first time since I came. You see, I am improving rapidly. I walked over 100 yds. & back this morning. I am gaining my strength verry fast, but I cant say yet what time I shall be able to go to Mobile. I want to be safe. I dont want [to] risk an other relaps, for I came near dying this time. I began to think you and the children would soon see me, but I should never see you in this life. It grievd me to know how much you would suffer if such should be the case.

I want you to write to me often. It gives me more pleasure to read your letters than evry thing else. Besides, when I see you I will tell you all about my sickness. I am as well cared for at this place as I could be, as if it you to wait on me. I dreamed I saw you and all the children last night. I thought you was all at your Pa's. It did not seem to me that we had been sepperated long, but I woke up and found myself here at Huntsville, 500 miles from you. What a sudden change. Oh, Emily, my dear, you have no idiea how bad it is to be sick as I have been & as far from the dearest Object this World can give, yet all alone, sofar as [I] was concerned, for nothing on Earth can give the comfort to the mind that the companion of the sick can give. But thank God I am again improving. I hope with care to soon able to go on my journey.

My dear Emily, let me again renew my solicitations. Will you not quit the use of snuff for one that loves you so dearly though 500 miles apart. What a pleasure it would be to me if I was guilty of any practice that was objectionable to you to quit it at wonce. My dear, it is for your good that I make the request. I would not deny you any thing that would afford you Comfort or Happiness that would not be an injury to you.

I want when you answer this letter direct it in this way.

Capt. W. M. Moxley

Mobile, Ala.

Commanding Comp. A,

18th Regmt., Ala. Vol.

I want you to write me about your condition. What change has taken place since we parted? I am so anxious to see you—never more so in my life. It seems to me it has been the longest time we have ever been apart.

I must close. I would write soon to the children, but I am too weak. George, be a good Boy. Betty, Laura, & Willie, be good children & mind your Mother, & Pa will Love you all.

> Farewell for a while,
> W. M. Moxley

~

[*Charles A. Thompson Beck to Emily Beck Moxley*]
Halls Mills, Ala.[35]
Nov. 22, 1861

Dear Sister,

I will write you a few lines which will inform you that we are most all sick with the measles, or a great many, though non[e] of the boys from our side of the [Conecuh] river is got them yet. A[llen] P[ridgen]

35. Hall's Mills, Alabama, the site of a turpentine distillery, was located nine miles southeast of Mobile on Hall's Mills Creek, a tributary of the Dog River, some five miles above the point at which the latter debouches into Mobile Bay and thus only that far from the camp of the Eighteenth Alabama.

is in the hospitle at Mobile with the fever, though he is mending now. I went to see him day before yesterday. He was doing very well and was well treated. The Dr. said he could come out to our camps in three days.

The Dr.'s company is in 2 miles of us now. We visit them evry day. Tom Shaw [36] is waggoning to Mobile. We can heare from their any time. [Charles A.] T[hompson] B[eck], R. W. [Reeves], [37] [and] J[ames] M. Stringer is well and doing well at this time. One of the Dr.'s men died the other day, and several of them sick yet.

The Dr. was left at Huntsville sick. J. H. Justice got a letter from him the other day. He said he would be heare in a few days. He had the chills and fever, but he had them break on him at that time or the time he wrote.

I am very well staisfied at the move to this place. We are 14 miles from Mobile, southwest. I expect times [are] hard in that part of the world, but we know nothing of hard times heare. We have plenty of flower, sirp, shuger, coffee, pickle pork, and beef [in] any quantity. I am greatly obliged to you for the gloves you sent me and A[llen] D. [Beck]. They answer the purpos very well.

I have written you several letters, but I dont [know] whether you have gotten them or not. I heare the mail rout is stoped down in Coffee, so I expect you dont get the letters I write to you. I will send this by Mr. Brunson, [38] as he is going back in a few days. It will [not] have postige as money is verry scarce. Some say we will draw money in a few days, but I think it doutful. The Dr.'s men have not drawed any money yet.

[Benjamin Thomas] Tom Moxley is in the Dr.'s company. I see him frequently.

Your brother,
C. A. T. Beck

36. Pvt. Tom Shaw of Moxley's company was detached as a teamster in November and December 1861.

37. This is Robertus W. Reeves, who served as first sergeant or orderly sergeant, as the senior noncommissioned officers of Civil War companies were sometimes called, of Company B, Twenty-fifth Alabama. Elsewhere in these letters he is called Rob and Burt.

38. This is most likely the father of Pvt. John Brunson of Moxley's company.

3
"How dreadful is war"
23 November 1861–28 December 1861

Weeks passed, and the Alabama brigade remained unarmed and de-
layed, seemingly indefinitely, at Camp Johnson. On 26 October 1861,
therefore, "due to the crisis at Manassas," Acting Secretary of War
Judah P. Benjamin ordered Leroy Pope Walker, still at Huntsville, Alabama, to "start Judge's Fourteenth Alabama to Richmond at once" and
advised General Walker "to come with your whole brigade, because you
cannot be armed by A. S. Johnston or by us." He held out the hope,
however, that the army in Virginia might be able to provide arms—
captured at Ball's Bluff—for his brigade. "You may do as you please on
this point," wrote Benjamin, "as I have other unarmed regiments that
will be delighted to get to Manassas."[1]

Walker demurred, still hoping to serve under Johnston in the West,
and was sorely offended at his disregard by the War Department that
he had so recently headed. From Huntsville on 1 November 1861 he
wrote to Johnston, commander of all Confederate forces west of the
Appalachian Mountains, protesting that he was "most anxious" to join
the army in Kentucky, having "declined to be transferred to the Potomac, where he had assurances of being armed." Beseeching Johnston to

1. Judah P. Benjamin to Leroy Pope Walker, Huntsville, Ala., 26 October 1861, *OR*, vol. 52, pt. 2,
p. 186.

aid him in arming his brigade, Walker assured the commander of what would become the Army of Tennessee that his brigade was "a fine body of troops, and they are well drilled for the time they have been in the service."[2]

By that time, however, Walker's brigade had received orders to proceed without him. On 29 and 30 October 1861, the Eighteenth Alabama took trains to Huntsville, by way of Atlanta and Chattanooga, arriving on 4 November. After less than a week with Walker at Huntsville, the Eighteenth and its sister regiments were ordered to Mobile on 9 November, again by rail, by way of Corinth, Mississippi, without their commanding general. Arriving there on 11 November, the regiment was detached from Walker's brigade and reassigned, with the Nineteenth, Twentieth, Twenty-second, and Twenty-fifth Alabama Regiments, to Brig. Gen. Adley Hogan Gladden of Louisiana.

"You must not suppose," Benjamin assured the bereft Walker, "I intended in the least to interfere with your brigade, or to divert you from your original destination without your consent." Due, however, to "the common panic existing South on the subject of the enemy's fleet" and the fact that regiments had been "ordered about right and left by the State Governors and local commanders," Benjamin felt that he must immediately order Walker's men to the point of greatest danger. So when Maj. Gen. Braxton Bragg telegraphed the secretary of war that he lacked forces to defend Mobile and requested two regiments, "to be armed with the arms belonging to the sick and absentees from the two commands at Pensacola and Mobile," Benjamin assented, believing it "better to make this use of the regiments than to leave them idle in camp."[3]

Certainly out of concern for the safety of this vital Gulf Coast port—and perhaps out of concern for Walker's apparent lack of zeal in arming or moving his troops—on 1 October 1861, Confederate adjutant general Samuel Cooper ordered Gladden to report to Bragg at Pensacola, Florida.[4] Gladden's new brigade was to become an element of Brig.

2. John Tyler, Jr., Assistant Adjutant General, to Maj. William W. Mackall, Asst. Adjt. General, Army of the West, Bowling Green, Ky. *OR*, vol. 52, pt. 2, p. 192.

3. Judah P. Benjamin to Leroy Pope Walker, Huntsville, Ala., 26 October 1861, *OR*, vol. 52, pt. 2, p. 186.

4. William M. Moxley, "Record of Events," Alabama Department of Archives. Special Orders

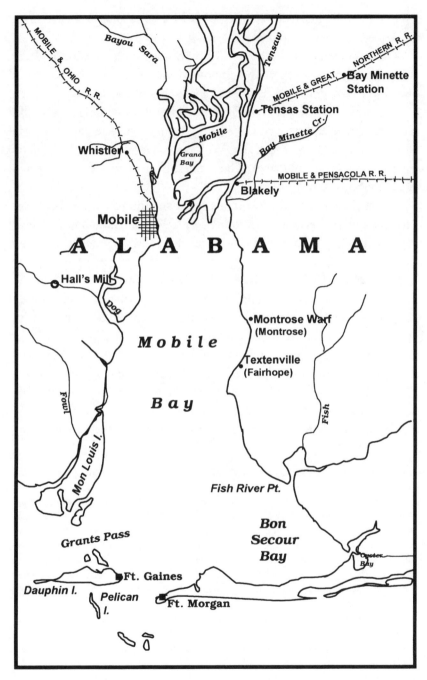

Figure 5. Mobile Bay, 1862 (map by Susan Young)

Gen. Jones Mitchell Withers's Army of Mobile of Bragg's Department of Alabama and West Florida.[5]

The Eighteenth Alabama, accordingly, was posted to Camp Memminger, ten miles south of the city on Mobile Bay, near the mouth of the Dog River. There the regiment, reporting 858 officers and men present for duty, practiced close order drill and performed fatigue duty. "In the virgin pine forests we cleaned off a number of acres of ground to drill on," remembered Pvt. Edgar W. Jones of Company G. "We dug up by the roots large pine trees. These trees, if in existence today, would make millions of feet of lumber."[6]

Walker, incensed at the loss of his command, protested forcibly to his replacement at the War Department, Judah P. Benjamin, but as Bragg informed Samuel Cooper, the necessity for removing Walker "from a position in which he was doing no good and so much harm is more apparent than ever" since his regiments were turned over to Gladden. Walker, he informed the adjutant general, had disobeyed Bragg's order to establish his headquarters with his brigade at Mobile, leaving it with "no head, no organization, no instruction, and no discipline," with the consequent "drunkenness and demoralization."[7] Indeed, the officers and men of the Eighteenth took the omnibus into Mobile on "pass" almost daily and, according to Private Jones, who later became a preacher, often returned to camp with contraband liquor.[8]

This lack of discipline certainly contributed to the war's leading

---

Number 168, Adjutant and Inspector General's Office, Richmond, 1 October 1861, *OR*, vol. 52, pt. 2, p. 157.

5. Withers was an Alabama native, a West Point graduate, and a veteran of the war with Mexico, in which he had served as a colonel. In 1848 he returned to Alabama to practice law and work in the cotton trade. At the time of his state's secession, he was the mayor of Mobile and soon thereafter was elected colonel of the Third Alabama Infantry. On 10 July he was commissioned a brigadier general and on 27 January 1862 was given command of all Confederate forces at Mobile. He was promoted to major general for his performance at Shiloh and later commanded a division in the Army of Tennessee until his health began to fail soon after the battle of Murfreesboro. Beck, *"Third Alabama!"*

6. George G. Garner, Assistant Adjutant General, Special Orders No. 14, 1 December 1861, *OR*, vol. 6, p. 772. Jones, *History of the 18th Alabama Infantry*.

7. Braxton Bragg to Samuel Cooper, 8 February 1862, *OR*, vol. 44, p. 266.

8. George Little and James R. Maxwell, *A History of Lumsden's Battery, CSA* (Tuscaloosa, Ala.: R. E. Rhodes Chapter, United Daughters of the Confederacy, 1905), 5; Jones, *History of the 18th Alabama Infantry*.

killer—infectious disease. Within a year of its organization, often before it had seen its first battle, the typical Civil War regiment—both North and South—had been reduced by a variety of lethal illnesses to 50 percent of its original strength. With the concentrations of tens of thousands of men—many from rural areas where they had never been exposed to contagious diseases—measles, mumps, smallpox, scarlet fever, and erysipelas swept through the camps, with devastating rates of mortality.

Especially deadly was typhoid. Although no figures are available for the number of cases or the number of deaths due to the disease in the Confederate army, statistics compiled by Union surgeons suggest that typhoid ranked behind only diarrhea, dysentery, and gonorrhea as the most frequently contracted disease in Civil War armies and was second only to chronic diarrhea as the leading killer. The *Official Records* report 75,368 cases of typhoid in the Union ranks, of which 27,050 proved fatal. Twenty-five percent of these deaths occurred during the war's first year.

Moxley's company was highly susceptible to this killer, as were his neighbors and kinsmen.[9] "We have a bundance of sickness in our Regiment & a great many deaths," he reported to his wife, and she informed him that her brother Allen was critically ill and that her brother-in-law, Fayette Stinson, was at the point of death, both with typhoid. It left the civilian community desolate, she wrote, "to see the poor Soldiers brought home a corps[e] and to see them that are sick brought home so low."

[*William M. Moxley to Emily Beck Moxley*]
Mobile
Nov. 23, 1861
E. A. Moxley

Dear Wife,

I write you from this place as I have arrived here this morning from Huntsville. I feel as well as I ever did in my life, though not as strong. I never mended as fast in my life after being sick as I have the last time.

I never was so anxious to hear from any person in my life as I was and am to hear from you. It has been 23 days since I have heard from

9. Brooks, *Civil War Medicine,* 6, 120, 127.

you. A length of time greater [than] I expected would ever occur without hearing from you. This makes 4 letters to you since I received any, one of them written on the bed when I was not able to sit up long enough to write. I did it to keep you from being uneasy. I am willing to do any thing in my power to make you happy, for without making you so, I could not.

I suppose I will see the Pike Guards to morrow. I have not seen my own Company in 18 days, but I heard from them one hour ago.

Tell the esq., Joseph [H. Justice] is well, but I left D[awson] W. Justice verry sick at Huntsville, but some better than he had been. I was detained 2 days on his account. I fear it will be some time before he gets well. As soon as he gets able to travel he will go home.

They are fighting at Pensacola now.[10] I dont know how long before our time. It may come soon.

My dear Emily, do write oftenr. Dont kep me in suspense if you can help it. I will write to you again in a few days. I must close for want of time.

My dear, believe Yours,
W. M. Moxley

~

[*William M. Moxley to Emily Beck Moxley*]
Mobile, Nov. 26, 1861

Dear Emily,

I saw Mr. Parker[11] this morning. He told me there was a letter on the Boat[12] in a box for me from you. I am anxious to see it, but I cant untill evening.

10. Rumors of Confederate attempts to seize Pensacola abounded during the war's early months, and five small engagements actually took place during the first year of the war. On 2 September 1861, a raiding party from the Union fleet burned the dock at the Confederate navy yard, and on 14 September, Union sailors burned the C.S.S. *Judah.* On 9 October 1861, 1,000 Confederate troops under Brig. Gen. Richard Heron Anderson landed on Santa Rosa Island near Fort Pickens, planning to break up Federal batteries in and around the fort. Union reinforcements, however, forced the Confederates to withdraw. On 22–23 November 1861 and on 1 January 1862, the heavy guns of Fort Pickens engaged those of Confederate Fort McRee. Moxley is referring to the bombardment of 22–23 November.

11. J. A. Parker was appointed acting third sergeant of Moxley's Company on 13 October 1861. He lost the subsequent election, however, and reverted to his former rank of fifth sergeant. Alfred P. Parker was a fifty-five-year-old neighbor of the Moxleys in Bullock.

12. This is likely the 130-ton side-wheel steamer *Bloomer,* which linked Elba to the Gulf of Mex-

I have seen Allen. He is very low, but mending. If he has good nursing and treatment he will get well. He is comfortably sutuated.

I am still improving. I want you to write to me often. If I had time I would write. I will send you 2 papers. Give one to the Esqr. Tell all the children I want to see them bad. I need not say that to you, for you know it.

> Goodby, my Dear Emily.
> W. M. Moxley

~

[*D. Newton Moxley to William M. Moxley*]
New Providence, Ala.
Nov. 27/1861
Capt. Wm M. Moxley

Dear Brother,

I seat my self this morning [to] writ a few lines to you which will informe you that I have rescieved your letters &, first, that I have since you writ to me to send for your famely. You [*word illegible*] to complain, but I think without a cause upon my part, for I did not know [*word illegible*] to [*word illegible*] for some time.

I regrit to hear of your bad health. I hope that you will continue to improve. I am glad to hear that Brother Thomas is with you & Mat. You seam prosperous. I shall be shore to come & take up my aboad with you now, as soon as I can aring my business & yours. I think that I can git ready by the time some of the boys git ready to go home, so you may count on my coming.

I want you to send me 5 galons of Alcohol by Mr. Beck so that I can fill one of my jars that they may be ready when I return, if at all, for I cant git enny in Greenville. Be shore to send it, & I will pay you as soon as I git thar, as I have not got the money to send. I want som for my self as it is all that I can do to git along for rhumitism.

Write me what I had better bring with me & so fourth. Give my

---

ico by way of the Pea River. On 24 December 1862, Union forces raided up the Choctawhatchee River, seizing the boat at Geneva and incorporating it into the West Gulf Blockading Squadron as tender to U.S.S. *Potomac*. *Official Records of the Union and Confederate Navies in the War of the Rebellion* (Washington, D.C., 1921), ser. 2, vol. 1, p. 46; Naval History Division, Navy Department, *Civil War Naval Chronology, 1861–1865* (Washington, D.C., 1971), vol. 2, p. 116; vol. 3, pp. 163, 165; Watson, *Coffee Grounds*, 236.

best respects to Thomas, all of the boys, & who I shall leave your notes with. I shall go to Bullock this week to sea to that dun.

Yours.

D. N. Moxley

~

[*William M. Moxley to Emily Beck Moxley*]
Camp Gov. Mo[o]re[13]
December 6th, 1861
E. A. M. Moxley

Dear Wife,

Thinking you might get a letter directed to Bullock, I concluded to write you a few lines, knowing if you are like I am, you are glad to hear evry opportunity. I am geting on verry well. I took cold when I came in to camps & when your Father was hear. I was not as well off as I had been, but cold is better. I am again on rising ground.

We have a bundance of sickness in our Regiment & a great many deaths. I think we have lost 15 since we came to this place. I dont think it is in consequence of the locality of the place. I believe armies will be sick any where you may put them, though they are taking Pneumonia. I have 3 or 4 cases in my Company, some of them very sick.

I heard to day from Col. Loomis' Battallion where Curtis' Company belongs. The man told me he saw 3 dead in the Hospital. One of them did belong to Harper's Company from Covington.[14] I asked him if knew if either of them belonged to Curtis' Company, but he did not know. I am afraid they will have a bad time. Their camp is so low & damp this winter. If it should rain much next spring, if cold, Pneumonia will be certain [to] kill many of our soldiers, & it is no respecter of persons. I hope to escape, for it is so verry painful. I dread it.

I would be glad to hear from Allen. I want you to write me word how he is geting on by [Charles A.] Thompson [Beck], if not before.

I know the death of Francis Jackson nearly killed them.[15] It is awful,

13. Camp Moore, named in honor of Alabama's governor Andrew Barry Moore, was located approximately one mile west of Mobile on the north side of the road to Spring Hill. Bergeron, *Confederate Mobile,* 13.

14. The Covington County company enlisted as the "Andalusia Beauregards" and was mustered into Confederate service as Company A, Twenty-fifth Alabama Infantry. Micajah Harper, the company's first captain, was killed at Shiloh.

15. Abner M. Jackson and Eliza E. Jackson were near neighbors of the Becks. They were the

notwithstanding [death] is of evry day accurace. Some where or other, this war has caused the sheading of tears enough if gathered to geather to float the great Leviathon in or babtise the whole Lincoln Army in, & some persons will be held by him who Rules & holds the destinany of all Nations in his own hands accountable for all the misary & reachedness their wicked hands has produced. I cant tell whos shoulders it will fall on, for I am certain a great many of our people an[d] those who claim themselves for us & even Officers of the Army are making this war a nother of speculation, and I believe some of it going on in our Regiment.

Dear Emily, I should be glad to see you here, but I see no chance. Your father can tell you how it is. You know how it is, but if it was not for your condition I would bring you any how & let you stay in camps. I would have to build a Shanty, which will be built for us to winter in.

They are buliding winter quarters for all the men. I think we will remain here untill spring. I am going home if I live untill the last of January. If I live untill then, my dear, try and be reconciled. Our fate is hard, but others is worse. If I was to go home now, I could not stay half so long nor neither could I go when I so much desire the time I hope to benefit you. If I wanted to go now, I could not, for I have no money. They have no money, as yet.

I intend sending you some as soon as I can get it. I think it will come soon, but I cant tell. I have bought a barrel of fine syrup, but I need not send it to you without the money to pay the freight to Mobile, but if they dont pay it soon I will borrow some and send it any how. I will say it will be in Greenville by the 20th, so you can get it home for Chrismas. If you need some coffee, I can send you some. It is 42 cts. pr. lb. Bacon, 25. I will try and send you some at the same time.

Well, Dear Emily, I dream of you and the children often, during which, of course, I am happy, but only for a short time, then to awake to find my self so awfully disappointed.

When I commenced writing this letter I did not expect to find enough to write about to fill more than 2 sides. Now hear I am writing on the 4 side after 9 oclock, but I must close.

---

parents of Francis N. Jackson, a private in Company B, Twenty-fifth Alabama Infantry. He was born on 6 August 1840, died on 26 November 1861, and is buried in the Spears Cemetery. Two of their other sons also served the Confederate cause. Warren A. Jackson was the overseer of Wilson B. Stringer's plantation. He was elected first sergeant of Company B, Twenty-fifth Alabama Infantry. He was named on the Confederate Roll of Honor for "conspicuous courage and good conduct on the field of battle" at Murfreesboro and was captured at Nashville, 15 December 1864. General Orders No. 131, *OR,* vol. 20, p. 936.

I will first let you hear Bill Kelly's sentence. He is to walk 30 days before the guard, ten with a board before his face marked on it "Theif." Then his head is to be shaved [and] his uniform cut off of him. Then he is to be Drumed out of Service of the Confederate States.

My Dear Emily, please write evry chance. The time seems long untill the last of January, but I look forward to that time when I shall be able to see you and all the children togeather at home wonce more, for I believe if I live, & you, and all the children, and we have peace as we desire it, that I shall be as happy as man can be on this Earth.

Give my love to all the children. You know you always have let me when I may.

Your Effectionate Husband,
W. M. Moxley
To E. A. M. Moxley, His Wife

~

[William M. Moxley to Emily Beck Moxley]
Camp Gov. Moore near Mobile
[December 1861]
E. A. M. Moxley

Dear Wife,

Your kind response came to hand last. I know you cant imagine how much happiness it gave me to read your letter. I did blame you for not writing to me sooner & more frequently, but now I hope and believe you are as much interested for me as it is possible for a man's wife to be.

My health is improving. I lack my strength, but I am gaining it evry day. You never saw me have such an appetite in your life. I eat as much frequently at one meal as I was in the habit of eating in a day. I neither chew tobacco nor drink whiskey. I think it is cause of my appetite.

You dont say anything about snuff. I am anxious to hear, puting as much interest as I do, for the dearest object to me on Earth. I hope you have quit it for my sake.

My dear Emily, you was mistaken about my coming so near when we left Huntsville. We went down in the direction of Memphis untill we got into Mississippi and traveled 250 miles through Mississippi before reaching Mobile. My dear Emily, I am as anxious to see you

as bad [as] an effectionate Husband could want to see his wife &
children, but I cant see, situated as evry thing is, how it could be, if any.

Well, I will take that back, for it would be of great satisfaction to
see you even for 2 or 3 days. The Order now for bids any person from
sleeping out of the Quarters, or at least any Commission officer, unless
in cases urgent necesity. I expect to go home about the last of January.
If I was to go sooner I could not stay so long nor in so important a
time. I hope you will become reconciled. We must do the best we can
& submit cherffully to that we cant help.

We are camped 11 miles from Mobile at as pretty a place as you ever
saw, and the finest sort of springs, and I think as healthy a place as any.
We expect to stay hear untill spring.

Capt. Curtis's Company deserves pitty. They have been at Fort
Gaines sometime, which was a disagreeable place. They are now at a
low flat place. I think [it] will be unhealthy. They seem to be defeated
and cast down. Some of them I hardly know. I am sorry for them, but
cant relieve them. I know they are dissatisfied. If their officers could
get well & go to Camps it might relieve them.

The Health of my company is improving. I have no bad cases at
this time. The 3 cases I last [had] died while I was sick. I am sorry for
Abner Jackson's family. To think their son left them in health and fine
spirits and now to return a Corpse is an awful thing. If it should be my
lot, I hope it may take place in the battle field. People become destitute
of the sympathy they wonce had. I have seen brother standing over
dying brother without shedding a tear, but I cant think it makes any
difference with me. I am ready, and feel as much bound to relieve the
suffering as ever I did.

I heard from Allen yesterday. Tom Shaw saw him. He said Tom
and Allen both said he said he was better. I hope it is so, but I am
verry uneasy about him, for, I tell you, he is verry low. I would stay
with him if I could, but it is impossible.

I want you to write often & let me hear the news of the Neighborhood. Since Jim left, we have formed a mess by taking in 2 of the
nicest & best cooks we could find. So we are doing much better than
we did before.[16]

My dear Emily, I must close as it is night and raining accasionally.
Please dont neglect to write. I intend to write to you evry opportu-

16. Manning David of Company A was detailed to duty as the captain's cook. Pay and Muster
Roll, Eighteenth Alabama Infantry, 31 December 1861.

nity. If I continue to improve as I have done I will weight 165 lbs. by Chrismas. I hope I may, untill I see you. I have not drawed a cent of money since I saw you, neighther have I any, only what I borrow.

Your Effectionate Husband as Ever,
W. M. Moxley

~

George, Betty, and Laura
Dear Children,

I want to see you all verry much, as much as Father could want to see his children. George, my son, you are the oldest. You aught to obey your mother and be good and kind to your little Sisters & Brothers. George, if you never see me again, never forget this, for it is from a Father that loves you dearly.

Bettie & Laura, mind your kind mother. Be good children so I may see how much you have improved.

Willie, be a good boy, & when I go home I will hug & kiss you both.

Pa's little Davis cant understand me. Ma, kiss him for me and explain evry thing to them.

Your loving Father,
W. M. Moxley

~

[*Emily Beck Moxley to William M. Moxley*]
Pike Co., Ala.
Dec. 10, 1861
W. M. Moxley

Dear Husband,

I seat my self this morning to write you a few lines to let you hear from me again. This will inform you that my self and children are tolerable well, with the exception of colds. I am taking a very bad cold my self. It is from exposure. I have been seting up night and day for a week, which makes me feel very unwell, but I hope I will soon get better when I get rest.

I think I shall go home to morrow or next day if Allen dont get any worse. Fate is very low. We have been looking for him to die for two days. Newton give him out yesterday, but he says this morning there is a little hope for him yet.

I tell you, Allen has had a hard time of it since he got home. He had fevers for 2 or 3 days though he has missed them now. If he could only get rest I think he would mend, but, poor fellow, he has not had any rest at all since he got home. There has been a crowd here all the time, day and night. That, and seeing Fate so low, keeps him distressed.

Well, my Dear Husband, you have no idea how many has wished for you to be here this week, Old Dr. Billie, as they call you. They believe if you had been here, the sick ones would have been well in this time. Sis [Mary Verlinda E. Beck Stinson] told me to tell you she would not begrudge one hundred dollars this morning if you was here. She thinks you could raise Fate very soon.

You would not know Fate now if you was to see him. He is reduced to a perfect skeleton. Newton says he has typhoid fever and his bowels is very much inflamed. Yesterday morning his bowels was of a dark purple color on the out side, but I do not know how they look this morning.

My dear Husband, you do not know how it makes me feel to see the poor Soldiers brought home a corps[e] and to see them that are sick brought home so low, and I do not know how soon my Dear Husband may come in the same way. Oh, the uneasy hours I do see about you. My Dear Husband, I dont think I could live long if it should be the case, for I feel like it would kill me and if it was not for my children. I had rather be dead than to see it.

This will inform you that I received a letter from you last Wednesday night, the one Pa brought. I was more than glad to get it, for I am all ways so glad to get one from you. I want you to write often and long letters. I sent you one by Capt. Curtice, which you have got before now. Pa says he thought he would write to you, but he is troubled so much he says he cant write now. He says he will write soon and [you] must write to him.

Well, it is now late in the evening. I will try and finish this letter now, as Tom will leave in the morning. You may gess how Ma feels this evening. She is in a good deal of trouble about his leaving. She is afraid he will be sick like Allen. She says you must do all you can for him, for her sake. She thinks you can have him taken care of. She wants him to get in your Company if there is any chance in the world.

They do not think Allen will be able to go back this winter. He has not set up any at all since he came home, and I cant tell when he will.

You wanted me to give you the news of the neighborhood. I tell you, it is very little I ever hear, for I never go any where to hear any news, and it is very seldom that any person comes to see me. I live a desolate life. Oh, I am so lonsome. No one cares for me, now my husband is gone. It is like I dreamed it was. I dreamed that you was very sick. I thought you would die, and I thought I was crying, and Bol. Stark[17] pass by me and ask me what was the matter, and I told him I was about to loose my best and only friend, which is so, for if I was to loose my Dear Husband, I know my friends would be few and far between. But God grant that I may never have that trial to bear.

My Dear Husband, when you come home I want you to come to stay a month, any how, if no longer, for I want you to be with me when I am confined, if possible. That will be the last of Febuary, shure. My time was half gone the 15 of Oct., if not more.

I must close, for I have nothing of importance to write. I will write you another soon after I go home. Jeames Willson from Georgia[18] has just come this evening. He says our connexsion are all well in Georgia. I saw Tom Thompson last night he was here.[19] He says he is going to see you all about Chrismas if he can get off. He thinks he will be sirtain to go.

The children all send there love to their Dear Pa and want to see him very bad. Willie can hardly talk about you without crying, and poor little Davis has to talk about Pa every day. He says "Oh, Pa, Pa gone, gone," and shake his head. You have no idea how much they all talk about you. Ma sends her best love and respects to you, and all the

---

17. Bowling William Starke was the first lieutenant and later the captain of Moxley's company. Born near Richmond, Virginia, in 1822, he studied law before moving to Tennessee, where he practiced until 1846, when he volunteered for service in the Mexican War. He served under Maj. Gen. Winfield Scott in the Mexico City campaign. After a brief return to Richmond, he moved to Elba, Coffee County, Alabama, where he was elected probate judge in 1860. He led Company A, Eighteenth Alabama, at Shiloh, where he received a serious wound to the neck. Resigning from the army, he returned to Coffee County where he again sat on the bench as probate judge on 5 May 1863 and served until 1868. He was replaced as captain of the Bullock Guards by Joseph H. Justice. Starke died at Troy on 5 July 1901. Watson, *Coffee Grounds*, 140–141; Brewer, *Willis Brewer's Alabama*, 589–705; Owen, *History of Alabama*, 4:1614–1615.

18. A James Wilson lived near the Wrightsville Post Office, Jefferson County, Georgia, in 1860.

19. A Thomas W. Thompson is listed on the 1860 Coffee County census.

rest of the family, and must receive a good portion to your self from your wife, one that loves you dearly, dearer than every thing els on this earth.

> So farewell for this time, my dear Husband.
> Your affectionate wife untill Death,
> Emily A. M. Moxley
> to W. M. Moxley

P. S. Newton has just come in to see the sick. He is tolerable well. He staid here last night. He says he will be with you in a week or two, any how. I will be glad when [he is] with you, for I can do as well with out him as I can with him, for he does me no good at all. He has been to see me one time since I came back from Auburn, and keeps all he can get from me. He has got some hogs to sell, and I have tried to get him to let me have some of them for my meat, but he will not consent to it.

> Yours as ever,
> E. A. M. Moxley

~

[*Sarah E. Moxley Brooks to William M. Moxley*]
Confederate States
Dec. the 14 [1861]
W. M. Moxley

Dear Brother,

Your letter came to hand yesterday, and I was very glad to hear from you, for I was very uneasy about you. I am glad to hear that your health is improving. I hope you will take good care of your self untill your health is good.

The family has all had the scarlet fever except my self, & I may take it yet. We have a goodeal of sickness in this vicinity & a great many deaths. Rufus Weeks dyed since I wrote to you. I was very sorry for him. He was sick a long time and suffering a great [d]eal before he dyed.

Jasper is hear. He has been to Augusta and is going to start home soon, and I want to send these letters by him. You must excuse me for not writing more. I must come to a close for the want of time.

May Heaven protect you and grant you every thing that you need is my greatest wishes from your true sister,

Sarah E. Brooks

Write soon as you can & let me hear from you.

~

[*Emily Beck Moxley to William M. Moxley*]
Pike Co., Ala.
Dec. 15, 1861
W. M. Moxley

Dear Husband,

I again take my seat to write you a few lines. These lines leaves the children well, but I am not very well my self. I have the worst cold I most ever did have, but I am able to be up, and I am at Pa's again.

Fate died yesterday evening a few minutes after 2 Oclock, and they sent for me this morning.

I left here last Thursday and went home and found every thing all right. I staid here two weeks when I was here. They have just left here with Fate to bury him. They will bury him at Spears grave yard.[20]

I will not go. Allen is so low that Ma wanted me to stay with her and him. He is very weak and has fevers yet. I am afraid he will never get well.

You have no idea how much trouble we are all in. It looks like it will kill Sis to give Fate up. They had to help her out to the gate, and Mrs. Jackson took her in the buggy with her. Oh, what a scene it was to see a wife give her best friend and never to see him again. She looks like she has had a spell of sickness. I am afraid she will give up when she get back. She thinks if you had been here you could have saved Fate, but, poor fellow, he is gone. He has paid the debt we will all have to pay sooner or later, and we know not how soon we may be called to meet our God, and we had better try and be prepared to meet him in peace.

I thought if it had been my lot to loose my Husband it would kill me. Oh, I am so uneasy about my Dear Husband. I am afraid you are

20. John Lafayette Stinson died on 14 December 1861 and is buried beside his infant daughter, who died in 1859. The Spears Cemetery, a rural family graveyard in southwest Pike County, is named for the Speirs family, whom it misspells and who were among the region's pioneers. *The Papers of the Pike County Historical Society* 2:6 (April 1962), 14–17.

sick. Do, if you do get sick, come home to your wife before you get too low, and let me wait up on you while you are sick. If you should die I would be better satisfied if I could be with you while sick.

This will inform you that I received your kind letter yesterday morning which I was more than glad to get. I received [it] on Thursday night, wrote the first day you got to Mobile. It has been a long time coming. I will send this by hand if I can. A. L. Shaw[21] is a going to start after Joe [Shaw] in the morning, and I want to send this by him.

I long to see the time come when you will come home. What a pleasure it will be to me. It will seem like a long time before the last of January get here, but we know not what will take place before then, but I hope nothing serius.

Well, my Dear Husband, A. L. Shaw has sent for this letter, and I will have to cut it short. They are waiting for it now.

Pa said he thought he would write to you, but he has not got time now. He has a very bad cold and Ma is nearly sick her self, but I hope they will all mend now.

I will send for Hanah[22] to morrow to come and stay with me. She said if I would send for her and send a waggon to bring her wheel and loom she would come. She wants to make cloth. I will be glad when she does come, for I am not able to do my work my self.

Tell Tom [Beck] I will write to him soon as I can. Give my love to Tom Moxley all the rest. I must close.

Yours as ever,
E. A. M. Moxley

~

[*Jourdan Beck to William M. Moxley*]
Dec. 15th, 1861

Dr.,

You must excuse me for not writing to you by Tom, for I had no chance to write, for we have been crowded to overflowing ever since I got home untill now.

---

21. Alexander L. Shaw was a twenty-eight-year-old Bullock merchant in 1860 and a near neighbor of the Moxleys.

22. Hannah (Beck) Babb, a cousin of Emily's, apparently moved in with her at some time during the latter stages of her pregnancy.

Allen has had a hard time of it. He has mended very little since he got home. There was so much noise & walking he could sleep but little. He still has some fever at times & a bad cough. I am in hopes he will mend when he can get the chance to sleep good.

We burried Lafayette this evening about sunset.

I will write more soon. I have not time to write now. Send Tom word how it is here as soon as you can. Capt. Curtis said he would try to get Allen a discharge. If he dont, I want you to try for him.

So I must close for the present.

> I remain yours as Ever,
> Jourdan Beck

~

[*N. Jasper Moxley to William M. Moxley*]
Louisville, Georgia
Dec. 15th /61

Dear Brother,

I now seat myself to write you a few lines to let you know that I and my family is all well, and I hope this will find you in good health. I have never received but one letter from you, and that was the one I got last night. I was glad to hear that you was improving, for I have been very uneasy a bout you since I left you.

I have nevr collected a cent that was owing to me yet, and I want you, as soon as you draw your money, to send me some.

There is a great deal of sickness in and around this community now and has been for the last two months. I am now at cousin Martha Cheatham's. Just arrived from Augusta last night, and I expect to start home this morning. I am now living at the Five Mile Station on the Central Rail Road.

I have never got a single letter from [Benjamin] Thomas [Moxley] yet. I ask him to write to me when I left him, and he never said that he would or wouldnt. You may give him my best respects and tell him to write to me. Give my respect to Leiut[s.] Justice and Pollard[23] and

---

23. Samuel J. Pollard was a twenty-six-year-old schoolteacher who lived with William and Emily Moxley in 1860. Pollard was promoted to lieutenant of Company A, Eighteenth Alabama, and was mortally wounded at Chickamauga, 20 September 1863.

orderly sargent and the rest of the boys. I will now present to you my best love and respect and close.

> Yours truly, your brother,
> N. J. Moxley

Direct your letters to Louisvill until I learn the name of the office. Hope you are all well.

~

[*Emily Beck Moxley to William M. Moxley*]
Bullock, Ala.
Dec. 17, 1861
W. M. Moxley

Dear Husband,

I again take my pen in hand to write you a few lines, all though it has been but a short time since I wrote, but I did not write half I wanted to write. This leaves the children well, but I am not well my self. I suffered a great deal yesterday and last night with headach. It was as bad as the spell I had the day I sent for you to come home from the store, only worse, for it lasted a good deal longer and I am not clear of it yet. I threw up a good last night with it, but I did not have my Dear Husband hear to give me any thing for it. For that reason I had to bear it the best I could.

Oh, my Dear, you have no idea how I feel when I am sick, or the children, and no one to speak a word of consolation to me. But it is worse when I am sick, for when I am able to do for them I can get along better, but when I am sick I have no one to do for me. What I dont has to go undone. No one knows what a time I have but my self.

God grant that we may live to meet in this life one time more. Oh, but we could meet to stay together as long as we both lived. Oh, but I could see you to day it would do me so much good. It seems to me that I can never give you up to go back any more if you should live to get home, but we must submit to our fate and hope for the better, if it never comes. But it does look hard for a Husband and wife to be seperated that loves each other as we do, or as I do, at least, for I know there is nothing on earth that I love as I do you my Dear.

I came home from Pa's yesterday evening expecting to find Hanah

here, but did not. W. Termon[24] went after her and she was sick. He
said she had Thyphoid fever and was very low. Mr. Justice got him to
go. He said he said he had to pay him in advance before he would go,
so I dont know now what I will do. I have been expecting to get [help]
but failed, so I am at my row's end. I shall be compelled to have help
from some sours, but know not where I will get it.

I have no friends that I can get any thing done for me with out
the cash—only Mr. Justice. He is the only person that will credit me
for any thing that I have tried, and I have went to him so much untill
I dread to go any more. I will do with out a good many things that
I need very bad before I will go to him for it. I have got the old
lady [Susan M.] Justice to have my washing done twice, which I
was compelled to have done by some body. I have went to Newton
several times to have things done for me, but he allway tells me to get
some[one] els to do it [for] me, and he has never been here but one
time since I come home from Auburn, and he has got all the notes in
his hands and has never tried to collect a cent yet.

If I had them I would get something with them. Justice said he
could get a hog or corn or something for me to go upon if he had
them. I want you to tell him to give them up to me—every thing. I
know I could do better by them than he has done, and then you give
me directions how to manage every thing and I do as you say for me to
do and how to manage about your and J. M. Stringer affairs so I can
understand it.

I think you had better get Newton to give me a deed to that land
you bought from Malloy as you dont know how every thing will turn
out. I have never mention it to him, my self, nor I dont want him to
know that I have wrote to you any thing about it. If he could give me a
deed of gift to it, it would be safe. Any how, I want to know if you
have ever had the deeds recorded. If not, it ought to be done.

I expect Mr. Priester will live on it next year. I want to know which
I had better take, the money or a part of the crop. He says he will give
me either and a showing for it. I want your advice.

Mrs. Justice has not been to see me but one time since I come from
Auburn. I am afraid there is some thing wrong about it. That is the
reason I hate so bad to go to Justice for any thing. I am afraid of her,
but I shall have to go to some body before long for meat or do with
out, one, but I dont know where I will get it yet.

24. William Termon was a twenty-eight-year-old farmer near Elba in 1860.

If I had been at home the last two weeks I would not have any now. I am nearly out of every thing. I have never got any thing since you got it for me in Auburn. I think it has lasted very well, but I am afraid you will think I have been to[o] extravagant, but I have not. I let Mat have some of my meat to pay him what I borrowed. They were out. Me and the children have eat a good many meals with out any meat.

Old George White[25] gave me one gallon of Sirup last week. That will help me along some. I wanted to pay him for it, but he said he did not want me too.

The old lady is very uneasy about Simon Godin.[26] She is afraid he is dead. She tried to get money for the old man to go after him but failed to get any.

I have a pair of socks for you. Let me know if you need them and I will send them to you.

My Dear Husband, I hate to trouble you, for I know you see trouble enough any how, but I know when you read this letter it will distress you very much and I am sorry that I have it to do, but I am compelled to let you know it or suffer or go to Justice, and I do hate that so bad. You dont know how I feel to go [to] any body els for something to eat when I never had it to do in my life. I have all ways had a dear Husband to provide for me and to [be] a head in every thing, and now I have no one that cares for my wellfare that is about here. My friends are all gone now that my Dear Husband is gone. They have all fled too, but I think I have one friend that will never forsake me while he lives. That is my Dear Husband, allthough he is far away from me to day, but I hope the time will come when we can be together.

I dreamed the other night of having a tent and thought I was camped with you. I thought I enjoyed it finely.

I shall have to close, though I have wrote nothing that will give you any satisfaction, but will make you uneasy. But dont let it trouble you if you can help it, for I will do the best I can and look forward for the time to come when you will be at home. Oh, what a Joyfull time that will be with me.

The children are all as liveley as they can be this evening. They are

---

25. George White was a Pike County neighbor of the Becks. He was fifty-nine in 1860.

26. "The old lady" is George White's wife, Sinai. One William T. Godwin, an illiterate farm laborer, lived on the White farm, and Simon P. Godwin, a private in Company B, Twenty-fifth Alabama Infantry, who died on 26 December 1861 at Barlow's Mill, is perhaps his son.

runing and playing in the yard. They know not what trouble is, and here I sit crying and trying to write to my Dear Husband, for I have shed lots of tears since I began this letter, but that is nothing strang[e] for me to do, for I cry every day and every night that comes.

The children all send howdy to you and say you must come home soon. So fare well, my Dear Husband, for this time.

Your loving wife untill Death,
Emily A. M. Moxley to W. M. M.

~

[*William M. Moxley to Emily Beck Moxley*]
Camp Gov. Moore
December 17th, 1861
E. A. M. Moxley

My Dear Emily,

I recieved your kind letter, which always gives me greater pleasure than anything else. But the information it brought me, of course, was of such a character that my feelings was different from what they have been on the reception of your other letters, though I was not disappointed to hear of the death of Lafayette. I greatly regret it, but we must learn to submit to Providential accurances, for him who rule the universe is able to kill & to make a live, so we should not complain.

I am anxious to see you & and the children & all friends, but if I was there to night I should not be as happy as I am. My sympathy is to[o] strong to be happy whilst others around me are in trouble. I can sympathise with Mary, but it does her no good, for her dearest object is no more.

How dreadful is war. Such as you have witnessed is of evry day accurance some where in consequence of this unholy war, seperating the dearest companions on earth, making widdows & orphans evry day, making the happiest homes desolate, turning joy into mourning.

My dear Emily, I am sorry for you. I know you are distressed, but I hope you will summon all the fortitude nessary for your situation. I look to the day when we will be happy again.

My health is as good now as it was when I left home. I think our Regmt., as to health, is improving. I dont think I have a case of sickness in my Company that is dangerous.

I heard from Thompson [Beck] this evning. He is not well. I expect to see him as soon as I can, which will be next day after to morrow.

I let Murrell have 5 dollars to him to give it to you. I have 146 lbs. of Rice & 25 lbs. of Coffee to send to you tomorrow. If you dont want that much Coffee, you can exchange it for something to eat. You cant sell it, as I bought for the use of my family. It cost me 45 cents pr. lb. The Rice will be worth 8 cts. pr. lb., cash. If you dont want that much, let Madison have it & tell him the price.

I may send you some other things, as I am going to Mobile to morrow. Let me know evrything you need and I will supply you, for I cant be happy & believe you are suffering. If I & you live one month & a half we will see each other again.

I am a fraid our Col. [Edward C. Bullock] will die. He is in Montgomary, very low. The news that reached us this evning was unfavorable. His death would be to this Regmt. like a father to his children, or, I mean, the death of a father.

What more can I write? It is late. I have written all I can think of. Still, it is so delightful for me to get my mind so fully engaged in thinking of you. I never know when to quit writing. Even after I have exhausted evry thing I have to write a bout, I still want to write more. I have no war news but what you have [heard], or will hear, before this reaches you. I expect to send some presents to my little children. Tell them how well I love them, and you take any thing you want and divide with the rest.

I want to write to your Pa, but I cant to night. If I have time to morrow, I will.

Our Regmt. was inspected to day. We was on the field from 8 Oclock untill 12. You may gess I was tired. I shall have my hands full now for a while. J. H. Justice will start home in the morning which [will] confine me closter to my Camps.

Joseph Harper[27] is sick also. He was worth a quarter to me. I hope he will soon recover.

My dear, dont you think I had better go to sleep? It [is] after 10 Oclock. I wish I knew if you was resting well at this time. It would give me much pleasure.

---

27. Joseph M. Harper was the company's first sergeant in December 1861. He was promoted to second lieutenant soon after the battle of Shiloh and was severely wounded at Chickamauga. *OR*, vol. 51, p. 16.

If you see your Pa before I write to him, tell him I shall write him soon and expect to keep up a regular correspondence with him.

I feel considerable interest for Allen. I do hope he will get well. If his Capt. dont get a discharge for him, I will try my hand & see what I can do. I think I can succeed.

Tell all the children I expect to see them the 4 day of February if nothing happens to me & them. It will be a happy time. If it could last long enoug, I should be as happy as any man living. If you need shoes for the children, measure their feet & send me the number of inches their feet are long and I will send them some shoes if I can get them.

It is very warm here. I have not seen any frost down here yet. All vegetable matter is green. Nothing killed by frost.

I must close. Give my love to all the children & friends, My dear Emily.

Yours as Ever,
W. M. Moxley

~

[*Emily Beck Moxley to William M. Moxley*][28]
Bullock, Ala.
Dec. 23[, 1861]
W. M. Moxley

Dear Husband,

I seat my [self down this] morning to write you a few lines this [*fragment missing*] you that we are all tolerable well. I am [*fragment missing*] but better than I was when I wrote to you [*fragment missing*], and I hope this may find you well and [*fragment missing*.] I received your kind letter last Thursday evening. It gave me great satisfaction.

Joe [Justice] is right sick. I heard yesterday evening that he was worse off than he was when he first came home. They do not think he will be able to go back in 15 days.[29]

Parson Rodgers was here yesterday. Him and [his] wife was on their way to see their daughter and come by and brought the things you sent me and staid until after dinner. Pa was here too. He came in the rain

---

28. This letter is sadly mutilated, with numerous fragments missing.

29. The 31 December 1861 pay and muster roll for the Eighteenth Alabama reports Joseph H. Justice on sick furlough. Alabama Department of Archives and History.

and it rained so much that he did not go home yesterday evening [*fragment missing*] turned cold last night and he wonted [*fragment missing*] hogs today and he started home about [*fragment missing*] before daylight this morning. He come on [*fragment missing*] see about going to Greenville after them [*fragment missing*]. I sent him word that they were there. He is [*fragment missing*] to get a letter from you before he goes [*fragment missing*] so that he will know what [*fragment missing*] he cant get them hogs for me [*fragment missing*] get them in two or three weeks [*fragment missing*] are worth 50 or 60 dollars th[*fragment missing*] and they only cost me 13 dollars [*fragment missing*] good trade if I never make another [*fragment missing*] what I shall do untill I can get [*fragment missing.*]

I am out of meat and out of money and cant [*fragment missing*] it with out the money unless I could get hold of your notes before every body sells all the pork they have to sell. Several of the men that were owing you had pork to sell, which I could have got if I had of had your notes or if Newton would have attended to it [*fragment missing*] not acted as you thought he would he [*fragment missing.*]

I am out of meat, or nearly so, for [*fragment missing*] get him to let me have one of his hogs [*fragment missing*] would not do it, so you [see] how it is, but I [*fragment missing*] expect to try him again. I had rather try a stranger. I shall have to try to get some from somebody. I dont know who to try but Mr. Justice. I shall try him first.

My Dear Husband, you dont know how I feel to start out to get meat and not one cent of money to get it with, and it looks like I never can get any [of] the money you sent me [*fragment missing*] Murrell. He would not let me have it. He said you loaned it to him, so I cant get it, and I have to get Justice to pay the postage on all my letters, and I have borrowed 2,500 dollars from him besides which [*fragment missing*] promised to pay [as] soon [*fragment missing.*]

You said you was agoing [*fragment missing*] to send me some envelopes and some postage stamps [*fragment missing*] have sent them. I have never got them. [*fragment missing*] perhaps they were like the money you [*fragment missing.*] Murrell would never have mentioned the money, but I got Pa to ask him for it [*fragment missing*] you the measure of the [*fragment missing*] have the money to spare, get [*fragment missing*], but if you haint got it to spare [*fragment missing*] to send me, besides let the [*fragment missing*] send me the money, for we can [*fragment missing*] fire and warm our feet if [*fragment missing*] something to eat.

I am very thankfol for [*fragment missing*] the things you sent me. There was 19 yds. of calico and 10 yds. of the woolen cloth and three yds. of Jeans and 3 oranges.

My Dear Husband, you dont know how bad I want to see you. Oh, but I could see my Dear Husband this morning, but, alas, it is all in vain.

Parson Rodgers complains heavy about [*fragment missing*] people not doing any thing for his family. He says they promised to attend to them for [*fragment missing*] but they have not done it and he dont [*fragment missing*] it at all.

My Dear Husband, you must excuse this short letter. Mrs. Singleton has sent to me for the flour I borrowed from her last summer, but I did not have it to pay her all. I let her have part of what I had. She has not been to see me since I come down from Auburn. Just as I expected. Well, nobody hardly ever does come.

I must close. Give my love to all enquiring friends, and, my Dear Husband, receive all the love a loving wife can bestow on an affectionate Husband.

> Yours untill Death seperates us.
> So fare well for a while.
> E. A. M. Moxley

My Dear,

You will have to send me some salt to salt up my meat, as I have none and there is none in the country to get.

I sent you a letter last week by mail.

Yours, as ever.

[*fragment missing*] send you the measure of 5 pair of shoes that [*fragment missing*] for all. The length of the paper fits George.

> E. A. M. Moxley

~

[*William M. Moxley to Emily Beck Moxley*]
Camp Gov. Moore
December 23d, 1861

Dear Emily,

As I dont feel sleepy, notwithstanding it is after 10 Oclock, I concluded to write you a few lines to night & inform you of our condition, which is deplorable. Our beloved Col. is dead. He died this morning ½ past 7 Oclock. You have no idiea how much I am hurt, for I believe he was my best Friend in the Reg^{mt}. Think of a person loosing their friend in my condition. I never shall forget the visit he made me when I was sick in Huntsville. He came to my room & seemed to feel verry sorry for my situation. He stated my Company would not only be benefited by my being able to go with them, but the whole Regmt. would be aided. I landed at Camp on Saturday night & he left on Monday. He appeared very glad to see me, and I believe he was, for he seemed to form an attachment for me. He always granted my requests & seemed willing to do so.[30]

I have not heard from Thompson to day. If he had been worse I should have known it. This is the coldest night we have had.

Joseph Shaw did not start this morning as I expected he would. Tell J. H. [Justice], I have not heard any thing from D. W. [Justice] yet, that is, since he left.

I want you to write to me evry chance. I want to hear from [you] often. I expect to have the chance to write often to you, and I will do so, for I believe it will give you some satisfaction to hear from me often, though I may make you tired of reading my hasty letters. If so let me know.

If Hannah is there, give her my respects & tell her I am trying to get William[31] off. Now I think I will succeed. I want him to improve his health, for he is a good soldier as is, for if he is well he does his duty without saying any thing.

Tell Hannah if you leave the children with her, to take care of them, for if any person would not take care of my children in my absence, & I knew it, I should never respect them in life.

> I must close.
> Good by.
> W. M. Moxley

---

30. Three weeks after becoming ill at Mobile, Bullock died at the Montgomery home of his friend Dr. W. O. Baldwin at 7:12 A.M., 23 December 1861. He was buried at Eufaula on Christmas Day. On 8 January 1862, the officers of his regiment appointed Moxley the chair of a committee to draw up a set of resolutions "to express our appreciation of his manly virtues, and our sorrow at the calamity that has fallen upon the regiment." The first legislature after the war named an Alabama county in Bullock's memory. Owen, *History of Alabama*, vol. 3, p. 255; Troy, Alabama, *Southern Advertiser*, 10 January 1862.

31. Hannah Babb's husband, William M. Babb, twenty-eight, was a private in Company A, as was his brother, Jack C. Babb. Both were on sick furlough in November 1861. Three of her brothers, Caleb, William, and John Beck, were also in Moxley's company.

~

[William M. Moxley to Emily Beck Moxley]
Camp Gov. Moore
December 27th, 1861
E. M. Moxley

My dear Emily,

As I have another opportunity of writing you a few lines to inform you how we are geting on. Sickness still prevails in the Camps. Some person dies out of our Regmt. nearly evry night. While at Auburn, when a person died some notice was taken of it, but now it amounts to nothing with the most of [them]. I am sorry we have to loose so many fine soldiers. Still other Companies are loosing 2 to my one. I have lost but 3 yet, while others, or other Companies, have lost as many as 10. Mine all died during the time I was sick.

I hope I will remain well unitll I can get home. I received a letter [from] A. H. Justice last night with Certifficate from Dr. Warren. I am supprised Joe [Joseph H. Justice] letting such certifficate come, for it is not worth anything. He states Joe [Justice] can not resume his duty before the 15th of Feb., which [is] 50 days from the time the certifficate was written, which is 20 days more than any surgeon has given yet, & Joe certainly knows that I cant do anything for a certifficate dated beyond what the surgeon would give at the outside. I received a certifficate from a Dr. in Elba stating that one of my men must have his furlough extended 4 months. The law says that a General shall not be absent from his Camp more than [*word illegible*] months. I must say that I [am] geting verry anxious to see.

A. H. [Justice] says I must send you some money. Well, my dear, I have sent you some. If I have not [sent] enough, I will send you some more. I sent 8 by Murrell & ten by Shaw, which [you] should have heard of. They had let you known it, for you could have sent me a letter at the time they did.

I read this dated Decem. 23 without saying one word a bout your health or the children, but, you see, they forgot I am getting verry anxious to hear from you. I cant help it. I want to hear you evry day or two. I want you to let me know what you need.

A. H. says I must send you a sack of salt. I dont think you need that much. Salt is so high, I dont want you to buy any more than you think you need, but I will buy a sack and send it to Greenville. You must do what you think is best. I know if you have recivd what I have sent to you, I think you can get on untill I go home. But if you need more let me know it.

I want you to send me William Henly's note. If you think you will need any more money before I can go home, let me know it. Tell Mat to let me know what he wants to sell in his neighborhood. I have not recevd a word from him.

I intend to give you a chance to live with out being a trouble to any person, for I dislike for others to sugest to me what I aught to do. I think you had best inform me what you need. You know I have always been willing to furnish you with any thing needed I could furnish.

I will close this for the present. If any thing of interest should accur before morning I will write some moor. My health is good except cold. I hope you are as well.

Saturday Morning, 6 Oclock, December 28th

As I promise, if any thing should accur I would write more. I have nothing of interest to write more than I have written.

If you was here now at our Dress Parades you could not help sheding tears, for I cant help it when I look at our Flag that Col. Bullock has so often stood before, now fol[d]ed up, covered in crape. The Drums that was beat to give the signal covered in crape, the Officers & men wearing crape, all because they have lost their best friend. Who can tell the value of a true friend in times like these. Their value cant be estimated.

My dear Emily, if you need any thing let me know it, for [I] expect to furnish it for you, let it be what it may, my dear.

I must close. Give my love to my children & my respects to my friends as to you. If you can dispose of my love & respects I desire it. You must reserve a plenty for yourself.

Farewell my dear wife & children, for awhile.
W. M. Moxley

4

"You have no idea how much trouble this settlement is in"

1 January 1862–7 February 1862

While stationed at Pensacola, Captain Moxley's regiment was placed under the command of a new brigadier general, John King Jackson. An attorney and militia leader from Augusta, Georgia, Jackson had been elected colonel of the Fifth Georgia Infantry soon after the beginning of the war and was posted to Pensacola, where he led a raid on the Union camps on Santa Rosa Island in October 1861. Promoted to brigadier general on 13 February 1862, he was assigned to command of a brigade of Alabama and Texas troops—including the Eighteenth Alabama —which he led at Shiloh. Reassigned after the battle, first to garrison duty and later to field command with the Army of Tennessee, Jackson commanded a brigade at Murfreesboro, Chickamauga, and Chattanooga, in the Atlanta campaign, and at the siege of Savannah. He was, according to Moxley, "a verry Tyranical man."

But as the war entered its ninth month, death and disease, both in the camps and at home, continued to dominate the Moxleys' attention and their letters. The fearful mortality of the hospital and the battlefield and desertion from the army became an issue, and volunteerism became virtually a thing of the past.

Soaring prices and shortages of food, clothing, and other necessities, too, began to take their toll on Confederate morale. The shortage of supplies created by the South's lack of manufacturing capacity, the blockade, and the government's unwillingness to impose direct taxes on its citizens combined to produce rampant inflation in the Confederacy. The Treasury Department's policy of printing vast amounts of fiat currency made Confederate money virtually valueless by the end of the war, and specie, a relative rarity even in antebellum times, circulated at a huge premium. By spring of 1865 the inflation rate was estimated at 6,000 percent. With his attempts to send shoes and clothing to his family frustrated by increasing scarcity, Moxley ruefully reported to his wife, "There will be no such thing as Calico to be had unless the Blockade is Removed."

With the consequent waning of martial enthusiasm, the Confederate government was forced, for the first time in American history, to resort to conscription to keep its ranks filled. In April 1862 the Confederate congress enacted the First Conscription Act, which declared all able-bodied, unmarried white males between the ages of eighteen and thirty-five liable for the draft. As James M. McPherson has pointed out, the threat of conscription served as a stimulant to recruitment, as volunteers could choose their own regiments and avoid the stigma of being drafted.[1] Even so, as Moxley ruefully observed, the rapid depletion of the Rebel ranks ensured that "no man can get a furlough now."

[*William M. Moxley to Emily Beck Moxley*]
Camp Gov. Moore
near Mobile
January 1st, 1862
E. A. M. Moxley

My dear Emily,

As I have an opportunity of sending you a letter, I never fail if I can to let you hear from one who often thinks of his companion far away. My dear, I have awfull news for Cousin Emiline & Mr. John Stinson and Family. I have jest learned that Robert Stinson was dying this evning. No doubt but he is dead before now. Is it not heart rending how often I have thought of you recently to know how uneasy you are?[2]

I understand that Capt. Curtis has lost 11 men out of his company.

1. Moore, *Conscription and Conflict in the Confederacy*; McPherson, *Battle Cry of Freedom*, 429–432.

2. Robert M. Stinson died of measles on 2 January 1862 in the hospital at Hall's Mill.

If it was the case with me, I should be sorry I came to the war, but I thank God I have lost but 8 as yet, & all my sick are on the mend.

I still have my hands full. Col. Shorter has been in Mobile attending to Courtmartial all the week, & I have to take his place. The last day of December was Inspection day, for to make out our muster & pay Role to be made since that time, & I have to assign Furloughs & Pay Roles which keeps me busy at times. I have double the labor of Col. Shorter when he's here, for I have to visit the sick. Being a Physician gives me much more trouble than other Capts. have. But I have the consolation to believe my men has been greatly benefited by it.

My letter will be shorter this time than common as I have nothing of interest to write. I have sent you and all the children a pair of shoes. If you have not heard of it, I expect they are at your Pa's. I am truly sorry you had to trouble the esq. so much, but I could not help it. I hope you will get your salt soon and the money I have sent you. If you think you will need any thing that I can furnish you with, let me know it, that is, if you will need before I go home.

I want one month to fly of[f] swiftly & bring us togeather wonce, but who can tell what one month may bring forth. It may seperate us for ever in this life, but I do hope not. I expect to get a furlough for Twenty days if no more, and I want you to be the judge & say what time that ought to be, but be sure not to let your anxiety cause you to have me come too soon for your good. I am as anxious to see you as it is posible for a Husband who loves his wife dearly to be, but notwithstanding, I am willing for your good to wait longer than the time I have set to go home, which is the 4th day of February. If you think I should come a few days sooner let me know it, but be sure not disappoint yourself.

I cant tell why Mat dont write to me and let me know if he has got all the goods I sent him. I have not heard one word from him since Tom left Pike. You may tell Tom I sent his med[icine] to him, but he had gone home.

I recivd both your last letters at one time. If I got your first sooner I might have sent more money by Murrell, but I thought of nothing else but he would pay.

I believe you had better let my Papers remain untill I go home. If the esq. will secure rent on my place, tell him to rent it, that is, I want him to secure cultivation. I will send you envelopes if I dont forget it in the morning.

My dear Emily, if you should get sick, send some person after me at wonce. I dont mind the expense, and the trip can be made quick.

I want, when you write again, [for you to] let me hear from Allen & Tom and all the family as far as you know.

I [don't] know what else to write. I must [close] as it is late. Thomas sends his Respects to you. Let me hear from you as soon as posible. If you could have a letter at New Providence next Sunday, [W.] Reaves could bring it to me. Give the children my love. Tell them if I and they live [I] will soon see them. I would be glad if it was not to part again.

> Your loving Husband, as Ever,
> W. M. Moxley

~

[*William M. Moxley to Emily Beck Moxley*]
Camp Gov. Moore
near Hall's Mill
Jan. 3rd, 1862
E. A. M. Moxley

My dear Emily,

As I again have an opportunity of sending a letter to you, I have concluded to let you hear from me, for I believe it will be some satisfaction to you to hear from me, even [if] it was evry day, especially if you could always hear that I am as well as I am and have been for some time. I have cold that anoys me some, but with that exception I have enjoyed as good health as I ever have in my life for one month past. I do hope it may remain so.

James M. Stringer came to see me to day & brought me a letter from you & your Pa. You may be sure it gave me much satisfaction to hear from you, but I was verry sorry to hear that you was so unwell. My dear, I want you to get some person to stay with you, let it cost what it would. If you cant get a white, get a Negro, and I will pay the money as soon as I go home. I dont want you to suffer for any thing if money can buy it. As long as I have but one dollar, you shall have it. When I see you I will provide for your comfort if I can get to come at the time which I hope I may, but I received an order this evening to prohibit any person from leaving camps, only on Special buseniss of an urgent character, but I think I can get of[f] if J. H. Justice will come back, and if he is able & dont do it, I shall think hard of him, for I believe it his duty as I have done as much for him as I have.

We are puting a Telegraph between here & Mobile. I expect we will remain here for a good while, perhaps during the war. I am certain this Camp will be occupied by some persons. I can [not] say whether it will be Yankies or us, for they are geting closer to us. It is thought there is a chance for a fight here after a while, but I cant say. I dont think the prospect good for a fight here in some time.

I must close. I have written this letter in haste as I had but short notice, for Parson Parker will leave from Mobile Hospital, & I did not know he was going to leave untill nearly 9 Oclock to night.

Tell your Pa he can have the syrup I told him he might have. If I had time I would write more. I will write by Mr. McWert. If you will send to your Pa's next Sunday, you will get a letter from me.

> Good by, my dear Emily.
> W. M. Moxley

~

Jan. 4th
Dear Emily,

I am up this morning writing by candle light. I am tolerable well this morning except cold. I have the Headache. Such a thing I have not had in some time.

Tell J. H. if he is able I want him to come back by the last of this month.

~

[*Emily Beck Moxley to William M. Moxley*]
Pike Co., Ala.
Jan. 7, 1862
W. M. Moxley

Dear Husband,

I seat my self this morning to write you a few lines. These lines leaves part sick and part well. The children are all well, and I am some better now than when I wrote to you last, though I have been rite sick. I am at Pa's yet. Allen is mending slow, but poor Tom is sinking as fast as he can. He is going just like Fate went, I think. I dont think he can stand it many days longer with out a change. He is not in his rite mind but very little.

I got your letter last night that you sent by Mr. Ammons,[3] and I told him [C. A. T. Beck] what you wrote about sending his Medisin to him, and he told me to write to you and tell you to come and come by Mobille and get a good supply of Medicin and cure us all. He said before he got so that he was sorry he come home. He thought if he had staid there and took Medicin from you he would have got well. But, poor fellow, I am afraid he will never get well. I think Pa has lost all hopes of him. He first sent for Newton and give the case up to him, and he quit him and left him with out Med[icine] or Dr., and he done with out two or three days and then Pa sent for Dr. Dyer,[4] and he has been coming here ever since Friday morning, and he keeps getting worse, and he has sent for Dr. Johnson.[5] We look for him this evening. If he comes and dont speake very favorable of Tom, I expect Pa will start some body after you in the morning. Tom is so anxious for you to be sent for. He says he thinks you could cure him if you was here. Pa says he dont mind the expense if he knew you would come. I told him I thought you would, and if he does send for you I want you to be sure to come. It is Tom[']s request that you should be sent for. I believe he will die if you dont come, so come if it is in your power to do so. It would relieve us all so much and do Tom so much good if you can get here in time. I think you can get here in three days.

I have not been home since yesterday was a week ago. I was down sick all last week my self, and I am not able to do any thing yet, but I hope I will keep mending. I dont feel like I can ever go back down to Bullock to live any more if I can keep from it. Mrs. Stringer says I am wellcome to that house that Murrell lived in, if I will go there. There is a kitchin and smoke house and a good dwelling house. I think now I shall moove there soon unless you think I had better not. I cant stay

---

3. William J. Ammons, the fourth corporal of Moxley's company, was detached as a regimental teamster in January 1862 but returned to the company in time to be slightly wounded at the battle of Missionary Ridge, 25 November 1863. He was nineteen in 1861. Pvt. J. H. Ammons of Company A, Eighteenth Alabama, was slightly wounded at Chickamauga, 20 September 1863. Pay and Muster Roll, Eighteenth Alabama Infantry, Alabama Department of Archives and History.

4. Edward T. Dyer was a physician in New Providence. In 1860 he was thirty-two years old and owned assets worth a total of $1,500.

5. Osborne I. Johnson practiced medicine at Mount Ida, Pike County, Alabama. He was forty years old in 1860.

where I now live, for no person ever come to see me. I lay there sick nearly a week and no person come a near me. I tell you, I have no friends there, and every person in this settlement wants me to come up here.

Jeames Stringer went to see me. He was here, and he persuaded me to moove up here. He told Mrs. Stringer that the neighbors ought to turn in and build me a house if I could not get one with out. So I think I shall moove up here soon if I can. I had rather have your advise about [it] if I could get it in time. If you dont come you must write soon and let me know what to do about it. I know I could not get to a better place.

Well, my Dear Husband, I will now write a few more lines, as Mr. Seamore[6] is a going to start back to camps in the morning.

Well, we are all on the mend, but my poor brother Tom. He is no better. He is talking all sorts of talk and picking the bed cloths. He is very much like Mrs. Parmer and Mrs. William in Barbour Co. I am sirtian he has Typhoyd fever. Dr. Johnson came last night. He says he thinks brother will get well, but, I tell you, I dont believe he will unless you can come and do something, and he wants you to come so bad. I do want you to come so bad. If it is posible for you to get off you must come any how. The hole family wants you to come.

I think Dyer gave him too much strong medicin.[7] He gave him 10 drops of turpintine over two hours and Leptandrin[8] and quinine[9] and crawly[10] and compasation and kept a strong pepper poltice[11] in his

6. Cpl. J. R. Seymour of Moxley's company was granted a one-month furlough in November 1861 to return home to recover from an illness. Pay and Muster Roll, Eighteenth Alabama Infantry, November 1861, Alabama Department of Archives and History.

7. Nineteenth-century medical thought focused upon the bowels, the kidneys, and the consistency of the blood. As forcing a stool or inducing a stream of urine were among the few results that a physician could produce, such procedures were employed with distressing frequency. Although the physiological effects of eradicating bodily wastes were undoubtedly positive, the cathartics, purgatives, and "drastics" of Civil War medicine killed far more patients than they saved. Brooks, *Civil War Medicine*, 63.

8. Leptandra is the generic name for *Leptandra virginica*, commonly called Culver's root or Culver's physic. Named after an early eighteenth-century American physician, the root of this perennial herb is used as a cathartic.

9. Quinine, a derivative of chinchonia bark, was primarily used in the treatment of malaria, commonly dissolved in a shot of whiskey. It was also erroneously thought to be effective against syphilis, rheumatism, neuralgia, diarrhea, and fevers and was promiscuously applied as an antiseptic, a dentifrice, a gargle, and a hair tonic. Brooks, *Civil War Medicine*, 65.

10. Crawley root (*Corallorhiza odontorhiza*), American coralroot, was, in the nineteenth century, used as a diaphoretic—an agent to induce sweating.

11. A pepper poultice was a heated soft mass, often of porridge or meal, heavily spiced with pepper and applied to sores or inflammations to supply moist warmth or to relieve pain.

bowels with terpentine on that. He had to take Medicin every hour and some times oftener, and he kept geting worse all the time, but now he is not takeing any Med. Johnson had the poltice taken off and cold wet cloths put in the place of it and gives him some sweeten dram to drink and stoped giveing the Med.

If you can come and will come to Greenville next Sunday night, W. Reaves will be there with a carridg, and he will bring you down to New Providence as he brings the mail every Monday. You must be sure to come, if possible, for I believe my poor Brother will die if you dont come and bring some Medicin with you.

And do come for my sake, my Dear Husband. If you dont come now I hardly know when for you to come. I dont think that I will lie down before the 15 of Feb., if I got my time out, but for the condition I am in I dont believe I will ever reach the 15. My time was half gone the 15 of Oct. I cant be cirtain about it, no way. It may take place sooner or not so soon. You must Judge for your self. I have wrote you all I know about it. I shall be compelled to get some person to stay with me, for I cant do any thing at all.[12]

I have not been home in better than a week. That is the reason why I did not get your letter any sooner. Pa sent me a mule to come up here, and I have not been able to go back, and now Tom is so low I dont know when I will go, but not untill there is a change some way, so if you send me another letter soon, send it to New Providince or to Pa's.

Mat says you must send him some brown paper for wrapping paper.

We received the shoes you sent us and was very glad to get them. They all fit but Laura's, and one of them was shorter than the other. The shortest one is a most to[o] small, but I think she can ware it.

You have no idea how much trouble this settlement is in. I went to John Stinson's Sunday morning, and such a scene I never wittness before in my life. I went in. Emiline was sitting on the floor by her Dear Husband's box and no one about her. She was crying aloud. She looked up at me and said, "Cousin Emily, he is gone." Oh, what an awfull time she had that day. So after dinner they oppened the coffin, and she started to it and saw him and she fainted and fell on the flour. They picked her up and put her on the bed where she lay all the evening. She did not go to see him burried. She would say, "Oh, God, my heart will breake." She cryed untill she could not cry, and it did look like she would die.

---

12. For a discussion of deaths at childbirth and fears of childbearing, see McMillen, *Motherhood in the Old South*, and Censer, *North Carolina Planters*, 26.

I must close for want of room. My dear Husband, you must write soon and often, and if you get sick come home to your loveing wife before it is too late. Besure to do this for my sake. Give my love to Thomas and all enquiring friend and receive a good portion to your Dear self.

> So farewell, my dear, for awhile,
> E. A. M. Moxley

~

[*Emily Beck Moxley to William M. Moxley*]
January 8, 1862
Dear Husband,

I again take my seat to write you a few lines. Pa has thought all day that he would write to you him self and I had filled up mine and he requested me to write for him. He says he is so distressed that he cant write in any satisfaction. He says you must come and come quick as posible. Come as quick as money can bring you. He told me he did not care what it cost if you could come and come in time. Tom is anxious for you to come, and so is all the family. Do come if it is posible for you to get off and quick as you can get here. We will look for you Sunday night or Monday night. Pa says if he knew you would come he would send some body to Greenville after you. He has told me to write this for him.

I receive a letter from you this evening wrote the 3 and 4 which I was very glad to get.

I must close, for it is so dark I cant see. I remain yours, as ever.

> Farewell,
> Emily A. M. Moxley

Pa has read what I have wrote and says tell you that Dr. Johnson says that he dont think there will be much change in 8 or 10 days in Tom['s] condition.

~

Jan. 9
My Dear,

I will write you a few more lines, all though I hardly know what to write, for I cant see that my Dear Brother is any better and I dont know whether he is any worse or not. Some think he is and some think perhaps he is a little better. He does not try to get out of bed as much as he did last night, but he has not got the strength, is one thing. If you can come I want you to come as soon as money can bring you.

Allen is still mending. All the rest are well. I must close.

Yours, as ever,
E. A. M. Moxley

~

[*Sidney A. Warren to William M. Moxley*]
Bullock, Ala.
Jan. 8th, 1862
Capt. Moxley

Sir:

It again becomes my painful duty to write you another certificate— painful to me because it is expected of your men to return when their furloughs are out, and my having to send them. Some may [*word illegible*] that I am first to keep them from going back.

Charles Driggers[13] has relapsed since he came home and is now down again [*fragment missing*] with Pneumonia.

Joe [Justice] is verry sick yet. D[awson] W. J[ustice] is mending verry fast.

Keep dark about my Mr. D[riggers]. You know that [Lt. H. P.] Walker nor [Col. Eli Sims] Shorter does not know any better, and I thought it was actually necessary to do so to make it legal.

I heard yesterday that Tom Beck was about to die. Abner Jackson died a few days ago. On the other side of [*this letter*] you will find the certificate.

Yours & c.,
S. A. Warren

[*on reverse of above letter*]
Charles Driggers of Co. A, 18th Ala. Reg. Vol., has relapsed since he came home and is now unable to return and will be at the expiration of

13. Charles Driggers was a thirty-two-year-old farmer from near Elba, Alabama, when he en- listed in Company A, Eighteenth Alabama Infantry.

his furlough in consequence of an attack of Pneumonia again. It will
be necessary to grant him further time to recover his health. The time
I would recommend to be as long as he may be consistently given. He
will return as soon as able.

Jan. 8th, 1862
S. A. Warren, M. D.

~

[*William M. Moxley to Emily Beck Moxley*]
Camp Gov. Moore
Jan. 8th, 1862
E. A. M. Moxley

Dear Emily,

I have the chance again to send you a few lines by Mr. McWert
who will leave Camps in the morning. I was in hope I should have
received a letter from you before now, for if I dont heare from you evry
5 or 6 days I become uneasy. You dont know how much I feell for you,
my dear. I am anxious to see you, but if J. H. Justice dont return before
my time, I see no chance for me to get off, if I do then.

Times is geting some what interesting. It is supposed we will have
fight in 10 days, but I dont believe it will take place that soon. If it
would, I could go home, for I know if the fight was over I then could
go home and stay much longer. We have the best place here for a fight
I ever saw. It would be almost impossible for the Yankies to do as
much damage here.

My dear, you thought if you saw something at Camp Johnson,
which you did see, what many never will see. But if you see our Camps
now you would see more. We have 6 or 7 Regt. all in a line & 40
houses built for the men with 8 rooms to a house. We have that many
for 2 Regts. The others that are now mooving in will not have houses,
as it would be too late before theirs could be built. Winter would be
over. We expect to move into ours the first of next week.

My dear Emily, I have been verry busy for the last two weeks. The
Field Officers has been absent, and I had to take their places. The Maj.
was off on Furlough. Col. Shorter has been absent attending Court
Martial in Mobile. I cant tell how long he will be absent. I think after
I have remain & attended to my own Company, as well as the Regt., I

ought to be entitled to a Furlough to go home once in six months. I shall do my best to get off, but if I cant, it wont be my fault, for I would make evry sacriface for you in prefference to any thing else, for you are always first with me.

Well, it seems strange, but I can inform you that Capt. Curtise's Company will be as near mine as soon as they can moove up as Capt. Brady's was at Camp Johnson. The Boys seem to be well pleased at the idiea of geting so close, but is [it] not strange they should when they had the chance to be with me all the time and refused? But it was because they could not see in the future. Mr. [Alllen] Albritton[14] is at my Tent now writing a letter to his wife. His son is very sick. He is in Curtis's Company.

He brought us news that Abner Jackson was dead. That family is in a bad condition now. It is a pitty. James & Warren is both in the war. One of them ought to get a dis charge. I shall get discharges for Allen [Beck], John [Stringer], Green [Stinson], & Jason [Stinson]. I have them on the way. I expect to have them compleat by day after to mor-row. The Boys may be thankful, for I have done as much for their satisfaction [as] I would do for my brother. I feel for the people in that neighborhood. If it was not for seeing my dear companion & children, I would not be back their if I could, for I know they are greatly dis-tressed, & sympathy would distress me.

I can say my Company is in a better condition now than it has been since we had the measels. I have no man that is dangerous & but one but what is on foot.

You see, I have folded my paper wrong, but I guess you will find all I have writen. I want to hear from you bad. The things you sent for, I will send to you as soon as I can. I cant go to Mobile untill one of the field Officers returns, which I hope will be soon. When you write let me have all the news, and make your self comfortable. You shall have any thing you want, if you will let me know it. I intend to go home in February if I dont get but 10 days, but I dont want less than 30. If I could get that many I would be satisfied.

If I dont get the chance to write in the morning before Mr. McWert leaves, to Esq. Justice, tell him the last Certificates sent by

14. Two Albrittons served as privates in Company B, Twenty-fifth Alabama Infantry. W. M. Albritton died of a fever at Hall's Mill on 14 January 1862, one week after this letter was written. McAllen Albritton was mortally wounded at Chickamauga on 20 September 1863 and died at Hill Hospital, Ringgold, Georgia, on 24 November 1863. Both were sons of Allen Albritton.

Dr. Warren was sufficient. Tell him to write to me again as soon as he can. I will write to him the first chance, but I have no chance at this time unless I get up soon in the morning.

My dear, I must close. Be in good hopes. I think we will meet soon, thow no man can get a furlough now, but I hope to have better luck. Kiss the little children for me.

Farewell, my dear

W. M. Moxley

~

[Appleton H. Justice to William M. Moxley]
Bullock
Jan. 11, 1862

Capt. Moxley,

I thought I would send you a short letter. Your family have been in Pike 2 weeks. I receive & took good care of your ½ of a sack of salt to day. Costello[15] will start to Mobile the 20 inst. with a full company if not 2. E. Mack, J. H. Brannum, J. C. Nelson,[16] & others near me are going.

Jo[seph H. Justice] can sit up a little. It will be 3 or 4 weeks before he can go to camp [*word illegible*]. He is very keen to be with you. D[awson] W. J[ustice] was taken down again. He took medicen, & I think will soon get about again. I think I will come down with Jo[seph] when he goes to camp.

Times are so dull I cant write a letter worth reading. Keep Jo. and D. W. J. offices for them. They will come as soon as able, or sooner.

People are bad scared here about a draft. Now, that will cause you to get some recruits this week.

---

15. Darcy Pierre Costello, born 22 March 1827 in Dublin, Ireland, was serving as probate judge of Coffee County at the time of Alabama's secession. He resigned to become the original captain of "Rabby's Independent Company," Company K, Twenty-fifth Alabama Infantry, recruited in Coffee and Pike Counties. He was wounded at Shiloh and again, mortally, at Murfreesboro, 31 December 1862. He died on 4 January 1863. Watson, *Coffee Grounds*, 138–140.

16. All three of these men served in Company K, Twenty-fifth Alabama Infantry. Pvt. E. R. Mack was fatally wounded at Murfreesboro on 31 December 1862 and died on 28 January 1863. Pvt. James H. Branner died sometime before 27 November 1862. Cpl. John C. Nelson was wounded at Shiloh.

Give my respects to Col. Shorter, Stark[e], Pollard, and all my friends.

> Truly,
> Appleton Justice

~

[*Joseph H. Justice to William M. Moxley*]
Bullock, Ala.
Jan. 12, 1862

Dear Friend,

I am able to sit up this evening. I never left my bed until 3 days ago. I can only sit up a short time now. D[awson] W. J[ustice] is sick, but on the mend. I will send this by W. J. Wasden. Your Bro. will start next Tuesday. Your family has been gone to J[ourdan] Beck 2 weeks. They are well, so far as I [k]now.

Capt., I have had a bad time of it. Nothing in the way of physic would stop my feaver. They told me that I had to wear out this feaver. To day is the first day I have missed it clear. [*fragment missing*] If I can keep from eating to[o] much is all the danger now.

Ben Carrol[17] is dead.

I think W. M. Babb[18] will make a die of it soon.

All the pork is spoiled all over the county.

Captain, I have looked for a letter from you, but, Alas, in vain.

Times are as hard here as mill Rocks. There is a great many people movveing about now. I cant tell when I will be able to go to camps. But as soon as I am able, I will come. Rest easy as to that.

I came verry near for getting how to walk while sick. I go like a drunkard. I must close and go to bed.

> Your freind,
> Jo. H. Justice

Excuse my pencil.

17. Benjamin Carrol, a twenty-seven-year-old Coffee County farmer, left a wife and four children, the oldest of whom was six.

18. William M. Babb was the husband of Emily's cousin Hannah. All three of these men—Wasden, Carrol, and Babb—were neighbors, each living within only one or two houses of the other in Coffee County.

⁓

[Emily Beck Moxley to William M. Moxley]
Pike Co., Ala.
January 13, 1862
W. M. Moxley

Dear Husband,

I know take my seat to write you a few lines. These lines leaves us all tolerable well in body but not in mind. Oh, my Dear Husband, what an awfull scene I have witness. My Dear Brother is gone.[19] He has paid the debt we will all have to pay and know not how soon it may be. He departed this life Friday night, a few minutes after 2 oclock, and we buried him yesterday evening about 3 oclock.

Oh, can you imagine the trouble we are all in? You have no idea how the poor fellow suffered before he left this wourld of sorrow and pain. He was not in his rite mind for seveal days before he died, but I have a hope that he is at rest. I think he has made peace with his God. He was seen to pray a good deal the night he died while we were eating supper. Mat and Robbin were standing by his bed, and he wanted Robbin to sing for him, and he sung "We Have Friends in the Land of Canan," and my Dear Brother began to sing with him and called the words and could sing the tune. I was in the kitchen and heard him and thought it was Mat and was surprised to learn that it was him, for I thought he was so weak he could not sing so strong, but I think the Good Lord was with [him]. He told them to look and see the little angels flying around over his bed. "Look, look," he says; "Dont you see them?"

He called for you that night and called several times loud and strong. "Oh, Doc, Doc," he says. He said he knew if you could be here you could cure him. It grieves me to think he wanted you so bad and you could not be with him. It would have been a great consolation to us all for you to have been here, but he is gone now, and you can do him no good, but try and be prepared to meet Him in a wourld where sorrow and pain are felt and feard no more, for I feel that your time will come next. But I hope it may not be the case, my Dear Husband,

---

19. Charles A. Thompson Beck died at age twenty-four on 11 January 1862. He was buried near his brother-in-law, John Lafayette Stinson, in the Spears Cemetery. *The Papers of the Pike County Historical Society* 2:6 (April 1962), 14–17.

for I think it would be more than I could bear, for it seams that I have all I can bear now.

But, Oh, it could be a great deal worse if the Good Lord thinks rite to have it so. Oh, if you could have been at the grave yard yesterday evening to have seen the widows mourning over the graves of there dear Husbands. There was Sis and Emiline and Mrs. Jackson. They went to the graves and sat down by them and such a sorrowfull sight. They poured forth there grief and sorrow over the remains of their Dear companions. It did look like they had all they could bear. I never have seen such a time in my life.

Pa thinks now that Dr. Dyer killed Brother. He gave him Lobelia[20] on Sunday before he died and kept him throwing up all day and such strain[in]g you never saw, and never gave him any thing to lick it, his straing, untill he become so nearveous he could not hold his head up and hold it still nor his hands, and he never got over it. I persuaded Pa to give him some soda water, and that stoped his straining so much. That was after Dyer left him, and on Thursday morning before he died he discharged a qt. of pure Blood and nothing els, and the same in the evening and began to sink from that, and he began to talk out of his mind Sunday night after he took the Lobelia. Pa thinks he tore something loose inside of him and that caused him to discharge so much blood.[21] I cant write all I want to write but I will tell you the ballance when I see you if I ever do see you again.

Sickness still prevails in this neighborhood. Louisa Stinson[22] is very low. They dont think she will ever get well. She has had the measels and then taken bowel diseas, and now they think she has Thyphoid fever. She is very low. I have not seen her since last Sunday.

I heard from J. H. Justice Saturday. They said he was some better. I dont have any idea [he] will go back to camps before the last of Feb., if then, so I have give up all hope of seeing you come at the time you have set.

I dont know what I shall do if you dont get home, and if you have

20. Lobelia is a common herb, sometimes called Indian tobacco, from which is derived lobeline, a poisonous crystalline alkaloid used as a respiratory stimulant.

21. During the second week of typhoid fever, when typhoid bacilli are present in great numbers in the bloodstream, the lymph follicles of the intestinal wall become inflamed and may slough off, leaving ulcers in the walls of the bowel. The dead fragments of bowel tissue may erode blood vessels, causing a hemorrhage into the bowel.

22. Louisa C. Stinson of Pike County was twenty-four years old in 1860. She was the daughter of John and Martha C. Stinson and the sister of Micajah Jason Stinson and Robert M. Stinson.

battle there you may get killed. I shall be very uneasy about you from this time on. You must write often so that I can hear from you as often as posible, and direct your letters to New Providence, for I can get a letter sooner from there than any where els.

I received a letter from you last week mailed the 7 of Dec., directed to Bullock. I want you to write and let me [know] where you intended me to get sugar from. You wrote to Mat that you had sent me some more than I would need, and I have never seen any marked in my name. I want to know if you did send any marked to me. I have got the rice, coffee, and syrup. Let me know what els you sent to me so that I may know what you intended me to have.

I must close. Give my respects to Thomas and all enquiring. The children all said howdy to you. Receive a good portion of love and respects from one that wishes you well in this world and in a wourld to come.

I remain yours as ever,
E. A. M. Moxley

~

[*Samuel J. Pollard to William M. Moxley*]
Camp Gov. Moore
Jan. 13th, 1862
Capt. W. M. Moxley

Dear Friend,

I write you a few lines to night though I have nothing to write. Stark has taken command of the Company. A young man by the name of McNabb[23] is appointed acting adjutant untill you return. I sent for the pay rolls to day by Capt. Hunley,[24] but he could not get them. They were not made out. I shall send again to morrow.

We heard this evening that Thompson Beck was your brother. Tom [Moxley] is very sick to night. He ws taken with a chill to day.

23. The regimental return for January 1862 reports Moxley absent and on sick leave. Clearly, however, his absence reflected the urgency of Emily Moxley's plea that he come home to tend her dying brother. Alabama Department of Archives and History.

24. Peter Forney Hunley was first captain of Company I, the Curry Guards of Shelby County. He was wounded on 6 April 1862 at the battle of Shiloh and took temporary command of the regiment early in the fighting at Chickamauga when colonels Holtzclaw and Inge were injured. Wheeler, *Alabama*, 114–116.

I received a letter for you, & Tom said he knew it was from Jasper [Moxley] & wanted to hear from him & broke it open.

Nothing of interest has happened since you left.

Nothing more at present

Your Friend,
S. J. Pollard

~

[*Emily Beck Moxley to William M. Moxley*]
W. M. Moxley
Pike Co., Ala.
Feb. 3, 1861 [1862]

Dear Husband,

I seat my self this morning to write you a few lines to let you know how we all are. We are well as when you left us, and I hope this may find you well. I have nothing of importance to write to my Dear Husband, for Dear you are to me. For I have spent some lonly hours since you left me, for no person is the satisfaction to [me] you are. Oh, I would be so glad if I could be with you this morning. It would be more satisfaction to me than anything els could be.

J. Stinson[25] got home yesterday evening, but I have not seen him. I am truly glad that they are discharged and that Newton is Capt. of that company. It will save you of a good deal of trouble. I have been uneasy about you ever since you left. I am afraid you are sick, as you had to travel all day in the rain the day you left me. I am anxious to hear from you now. I want you to be carefull and take good care of your self, and if you get sick I want you to come home to me, for I do not know when I will be able to go to my Dear Husband.

If there is any chance in the world for you to get a furlow to come home the last of Feb., I want you to come. For my sake, do please come, for I dont feel like I could go through with what I shall have to bear without my Dear Husband. If you come I will be a thousand times thankfull to you for that kind favor. I think you can get a furlow, for I believe you can accomplish any thing you under take, for it seams

25. Joseph Franklin Stinson, a twenty-four-year-old Pike County farmer in 1860, was the son of Micajah B. and Sarah J. Stinson and the husband of Adeline Stinson. He served as a private in Company B, Twenty-fifth Alabama Infantry.

that God is on your side, for it does not make any diference how many is against you, you allways gain the victory.

Well, now for something els. Mrs. Stinson and Emiline[26] has sent me a peice to put in this letter for them, and Emiline said if you did not have the money to spare to get them things with, as soon as Newton's company drawed theire money to take that and get them with it, but if you did have the money, to send them as soon as you could. Hannah [Babb] wants you to send her 12 yds. of sollid Black calico, and Sis says send her 10 yds. of Black Muslin, and if you could get a fine bonnett for 4 or 5 dollars (a mourning bonnett) to get her one, and if you could not, to get her 2 yds. of ginghams Black, and she said she would pay me the money for them as soon as she got it. If you send these things, write to me what they all cost and the frieght on them so that I may know how to let them go, and you may do as you think best about the things you spoke about sending me, for I had rather have your choice than my own, just what ever you think will suit me best. So enough of that.

I went to Pa's yesterday and spent the day. All the children was there but you, but still it was the most desalate looking day I ever saw. Pa and Ma, Sis, Mat and Mary[27] come home with me to hear the news from Mobile, and staid untill bed time.

I must come to a close. Give my love to all inquiring friends. The children all send howdy to you and talk about you. I shall never forget the last Wednesday night you spent with me—how you done that night before going to bed. You walked round and stood and look at the children all a good while and then lay down side of little Davis and huged and kiss him and he a sleep. I am afraid it will be the last time. Pa wants Davis called Tompson Davis.[28]

> So farwell, my Dear Husband, for a while.
> Yours untill Death,
> E. A. Moxley

26. Martha C. Stinson, wife of John L. Stinson, was forty-five years old in 1860. Emiline was married to their son, Robert M. Stinson, who had died in the hospital at Hall's Mill on 2 January 1862.

27. Mary M. (Stringer) Beck of Pike County was eighteen years old in 1860. She was the daughter of Wilson B. Stringer and Margaret Ann (Williamson) Stringer and was married to Emily's brother, Madison L. (Mat) Beck.

28. This change of name was made in memory of Jourdan Beck's son and Emily's brother, Charles A. Thompson Beck, who died on 11 January 1862.

~

[*William M. Moxley to Emily Beck Moxley*]
Camp Memminger[29]
Feb. 5, 1862
E. A. M. Moxley

Dear Emily,

I could not write more in Mobile than the Boys could tell you. I had so much to do it kept me busy all day, but I gained the [*word illegible*] as you have been informed before now. I am glad enough of it, but I dont believe evry person is, so I am still busy writing discharges or application for them.

I found S. J. Pollard suffering with Ærysaepuly[30] in his face, but he is mending. I found some of my Boys verry sick, but not dangerous. The most of them are able to drill.

Newton is Capt., of Company (B) 25 Regt., as you have been informed. I expect to get his Company transfered to our Regt. I am satisfied we can succeed. I shall commence opperations to morrow. I shall be glad when I get through with my undertakings.

I am anxious about you. Keep me posted, and as soon as you can, I shall look for you to come. I do hope to hear of your case resulting well. You dont know how much anxiety I feel about you.

Tell Mat to send me a load of Chickens & Eggs, for we need them.

Bill Kelly was drumed out camps before I came. I understand some of the soldiers of an other Regt. followed after him & kept knocking off his hat to expose his Bald head, and he killed one or stabed him so he has since died.

I think from evry circumstance we will remain here for some time, perhaps as long as the war lasts. The health of our Regt. is much better than it has been since we left Auburn. I was told by Dr. Barnette[31] to

29. Camp Memminger, on Mobile Bay, near the mouth of the Dog River, ten miles south of Mobile, was named in honor of Confederate Secretary of the Treasury Christopher Gustavus Memminger.

30. Erysipelas was an eruptive fever that, although ordinarily affecting only children, reached epidemic proportions in Confederate and Union armies, especially during the first year of the war. Brooks, *Civil War Medicine*, 120.

31. Dr. J. R. Barnett was regimental surgeon of the Eighteenth Alabama. He was captured at Shiloh but after his exchange was transferred in March 1864 to the staff of Brig. Gen. James Ronald Chalmers and on 3 June 1864 became chief surgeon of Chalmers's division. *Staff Officers of the Confederate States Army*, 10.

day that only 2 men [have died] in the entire Regt. in 3 week, while they still die in Loomis['s].

Tell your Pa to write to me often. Tell them all to write. It gives me great satisfaction to hear from those I love.

I dont know of anything more I can write that would interest you. Tell Allen he must make haste & come back to fix up his papers so his money can be drawed, though Curtis's Company has not been Paid of[f] yet, and I dont know when they will.

Give my love to those whom I love, which will enclude the children, you know. Tell George I will write to him before long, so he must learn to read my letters & to write to me. I must close for want of something to write to you.

I am your effectionate
W. M. Moxley

William A. Kelly, the soldier who stole Moxley's wallet, was under arrest by sentence of a court-martial in December 1861. Edgar W. Jones described his subsequent drumming out in his memoir of the Eighteenth Alabama. "A great crowd of men followed the procession. And when the limit of the camp was reached the guard turned back, but not so with the crowd, especially the base sort. They followed the poor fellow and would run up and kick him and knock his hat off and otherwise abuse him. Finally a man stepped up and handed the thief a knife and told him to defend himself. He finally turned on his tormentors and stabbed two, one so severely that he died in a few days from the wound. The thief then took to the march and this writer has never heard of him since."[32]

[*William M. Moxley to Emily Beck Moxley*]
Camp Memenger
Feb. 7th, 1862
E. A. M. Moxley

My dear Emily,

I again write you a few lines because I can enjoy myself better writing to you than any other way. I am anxious to hear from you & shall remain so untill I do. Your condition makes me more so.

32. Pay and Muster Roll, Eighteenth Alabama Infantry, December 1861, Alabama Department of Archives and History; Jones, *History of the 18th Alabama Infantry*.

I am well. My company is well, except 3 men. They are not dangerous. We have better health in our Regiment than any other. We have a new General, some say a verry Tyranical man. I cant say all I know.

Esq. Justice carried D. W. Justice application for discharge to the rong place, & he supposed I did it & spoke of punishing me for it.

When I see how much difference in the officers of the present day & the old Revolution, it does in some degree shake my faith in our success. There cannot be any simularity if Hystory gives us a correct an account.

I understand Col. Lumis is very Rathy in consequence of my having the boys discharged. He told Newton they should never draw any pay. I have no doubt but he will do his best to keep them from it. I believe it. It is an evedence of his true character.

I cant write you a long letter for want of something to write. I am anxious to see the day come when you can come & visit us. I am willing to pay your board as long as you can stay. I can save enough by being more saving than I have been to pay your board.

It expected we will still have a fight here. General Bragg has movd to Mobile. They must be anticipating an attact on Mobile or he would not have moved down here.[33] Some think if we can hold our hand 60 days longer there will be a great change in our situation.

I have sent some black bombisin[34] which will make you [a] good dress. It will be worth 60 cts. pr. yard. I have sent some other things: some homespun [and] some osnaburg,[35] which will be worth 25 cts. pr. yard. You take such things as you need & let Mat sell the balance. I will send him a bill of them, so he can [k]no[w] what to ask for them, though such things are rising evry day. Apple[ton] can sell Black Calico cheaper now than they will in Mobile. Common black is worth 30 cts., and Calico such as Justice sold at 10 cts. is now worth 25 cts. here. There will be no such thing as Calico to be had unless the Blockade is Removed.

I intend to quit drinking any thing to save money to pay your

---

33. On 7 March 1861, Braxton Bragg, formerly a lieutenant colonel in the U.S. Army, was appointed a brigadier general and was given command of all Confederate forces in the Mobile-Pensacola area. His change of base in February 1862 was designed not, as Captain Moxley supposed, to defend Mobile but to evacuate it in response to Federal gains in Kentucky and Tennessee, and on 28 February 1862 he departed for Corinth, Mississippi, with 10,000 troops from the Gulf Coast garrisons. McWhiney, *Braxton Bragg and the Confederate Defeat*, 202.

34. Bombazine is silk fabric of a twill weave, dyed black for mourning wear.

35. Osnaburg was a coarse, durable fabric of plain cotton weave.

board, for your company would be worth more to me than whiskey. To drink it, I could get it for nothing.[36]

I think we will remain here for some time, perhaps as long as the war lasts. I hope we will, for I think this to be as healthy a place as any. I think if you was well & here you would delighted.

I will close for the present. If any thing happens between this and morning, I will write to you some more. If not, give my best wishes to all your Pa's family, to all my friends, to the children, & Hannah [Babb]. Little Davis will now understand when you tell him about me. Talk to them all. Tell them to be good children for my sake. I want to see them good when I return, for I do hope the war may close so we can remain at home togeather the remainder of our lives. I think we could enjoy ourselves much better than we ever did.

I understand our camp is still enlarging. I have sent you some very wide shirting. You had better keep it & let Mat sell the balance. I wish I could only hear from you evry day. If I could I would be better satisfied.

> I must close for the present.
> Your Effectionate Husband,
> W. M. Moxley

～

Dear Emily,

Nothing new has turned since writing this evening. It [is] now [after] Role Call, but I dont feel like going to bed, & while I am thinking about you I have concluded to send you Seventeen Dollars in gold to take of[f] for me by A. H. Justice. I shall send some things by him in a little trunk. You can sell the trunk for $2.50 if you dont want it. If you dont want what is in the trunk, let Mat sell them. Such things will be out of reach soon. If you need any thing I have not sent, you let me know it.

We have a bundance of rain & warm weather here now.

Tell Hannah her Brothers are both well. I found S. J. Pollard with Errysepulus, as I wrote to you by Mr. King,[37] but he is about well now.

I will enclose the bills of what I bought in this letter. You can give

36. U.S. Army regulations, copied by the Confederacy, authorized a daily one-gill whiskey ration "in case of excessive fatigue and exposure." War Department, *Revised Regulations*, 244.

37. Seven men named King served in Company B, Twenty-fifth Alabama Infantry.

them to Mat. You need not show them. Tell Mat he must make them pay, for I cant buy any more at that price. Molasses is now worth 42 cts. Tell him I will write to him by the next mail.

Yours, as ever,
W. M. Moxley

I hope you are well.
Tell Mat I think the brown shirting cost 22 cts.

5

"Oh, what a sudden death"

10 February 1862–25 February 1862

The winter of 1861–1862 was a time of disaster for the Confederate cause. On 6 February 1862, with the approach of Maj. Gen. Ulysses S. Grant's forces, Brig. Gen. Lloyd Tilghman's 3,400-man garrison evacuated Fort Henry, opening the Tennessee River to incursion by Union gunboats as far upstream as Mussel Shoals, Alabama. Ten days later, after a four-day battle and siege, Confederate generals John B. Floyd, Gideon J. Pillow, and Simon Bolivar Buckner surrendered Fort Donelson to Grant's army. The fall of this strategically vital fortress on the Cumberland River, with its 12,000-man garrison, not only materially weakened Gen. Albert Sidney Johnston's Army of Tennessee but made inevitable the loss of all of Kentucky as well as central and western Tennessee to the South.[1]

With the armies of U.S. Grant and Don Carlos Buell fast approaching, the Confederate position at Nashville became untenable, and the city was abandoned by the state government, as well as by many of its citizens, on 16 February. On 20 February, Johnston's outflanked and outnumbered army evacuated the city, falling back on Murfreesboro, and

---

1. Cooling, *Forts Henry and Donelson.*

on 25 February, Buell's army occupied the Tennessee capital and the most vital manufacturing center in the western Confederacy.

This series of debacles inspired Confederate politicians to question the competence of their military leadership—particularly the process by which officers were chosen and promoted. The practice of electing company-grade officers and then promoting them by seniority as vacancies occurred in their companies and regiments was called into question, thus jeopardizing the recent commissioning of William Moxley's brother Daniel Newton Moxley as captain of Company B, Twenty-fifth Alabama Infantry.

Jefferson Davis advised the Senate and House of Representatives of the Confederate States that, rather than promote or allow the election of incompetent company-grade officers, the two chambers should pass legislation that would strengthen the leadership of the army by consolidating understrength companies and transferring officers from depleted veteran companies to companies of fresh recruits. Davis advised Congress that advancement of officers "incompetent to fill vacancies" had failed to provide the quality of discipline and leadership required to maintain an effective military force and that "tender consideration for worthless and incompetent officers is but another name for cruelty toward the brave men who fall sacrifices to these defects of their leaders." Davis's proposal went unheeded, however, and untried officers such as Daniel Newton Moxley continued to lead companies.[2]

Of much greater concern to Emily Moxley that February, however, were her advancing pregnancy and her mistrust of such medical care as she might expect from the local physician; the death of a near neighbor and friend in childbirth; and the apparent theft of her hogs—her family's sole food resource for the coming year.

"For nearly all middle- and upper-class women," Sally G. McMillen concluded, "a persistent fear of childbirth clouded the anticipation of a new son or daughter."[3] In antebellum America, frequent pregnancies, barbaric medical practice, and a plague of both endemic and epidemic illnesses conspired to produce a shocking rate of maternal and infant

2. Richardson, *A Compilation*, 1:257–258.
3. McMillen, *Motherhood in the Old South*, 25, 81, 84.

mortality. The South had an unhealthful climate, families larger than
the national norm—an average of 5.5 live children were borne by Alabama plantation wives during the antebellum period—and an agrarian
lifestyle known for its lonely isolation. As a consequence, the South suffered from a higher maternal mortality rate than any other settled region of the country. Indeed, as 1850 federal census data reveal, approximately one out of twenty-five white women in the South who died in
that year died in childbirth, twice the maternal mortality rate in New
England and the Middle Atlantic states.[4]

Constant fear of death—of both mother and child—coupled with
the certainty of suffering in the absence of a loving and supportive
group of family and friends naturally negatively affected a woman's at-
titude toward childbirth, a circumstance that in itself contributed to the
danger and pain of the experience. Emily Moxley was certainly beset
with all of these travails and seems a special subject of God's promise to
"greatly multiply thy sorrow and thy conception; in sorrow thou shalt
bring forth thy children." Yet, as she assured her husband, "I live in hope
if I die in despare."

[*Emily Beck Moxley to William M. Moxley*]
Pike Co., Ala.
Feb. 10, 1862
W. M. Moxley

Dear Husband,

I again take my seat to write you a few lines with out geting a line
from you. This leaves us all tolerable well, and I hope it may find you
the same, all though I am very uneasy about you. I have dreamed of
being with you nearly every night since you left, and I understand that
there is a great confusion down there among some of you that keeps
me very uneasy about my Dear Husband. I want you to write often. I
thought sure I would get a letter when John Stringer got home, but
was sadly disappointed.

I have nothing of importance to write. Jack Shaw has lost his wife.[5]

---

4. McMillen, *Motherhood in the Old South*, 1–4, 32.

5. These are the Becks' neighbors Andrew Jackson Shaw and his wife, Sarah Ann. She was
twenty-eight years old and left two children under the age of five.

She died last Monday night. She expected to be confined in two weeks. She was taken on Monday morning with flooding[6] and sent for Dr. Willis, and he could not stop it and she died Monday night about 8 oclock. Her child was never borned.

Oh, what a suden death. I am sorry for Mr. Shaw to think that she [was] well Sunday night and died Monday night. You see, there is no Dr. here that is worth any thing. I think if you had been with her you could have saved her.

That is the Dr. you wanted me to have. What confidence can I have in him? None at all. You see my chance, and again I will persuade you to come if it is in your power to do so, for nothing on earth would give me the satisfaction that your comeing would give. Do, my Dear Husband, come.[7]

I heard that 4 privetes and one commision officer could leave a company at once, and I think you can get off. I hate to beg you so hard to do any thing, but I cant help it this time and be reconciled to my fate. But if you cant come, I hope God will be with me and bear me up in my troubles, and if we never meet in this wourld, I hope we may meet in a better wher parting will be no more.

~

[*Emily Beck Moxley to William M. Moxley*]
Feb. 11[, 1862]

Dear Husband,

We are all well this evening. I saw J. Stringer just now, and he is going over the river, and I have not got time to write much. I received a letter from you to day, wrote the 3 [February], which I was very glad to get but did not give me any satisfaction about your comming home soon, but I hope you will change your notions when you get this.

We have cold weather now. Pa has found one of my hogs to day and killed it and has gone back to the swamp to hunt the others.

6. "Flooding" is a copious bleeding of the uterus. For a discussion of the causes and treatment of hemorrhaging during childbirth in the antebellum South, see McMillen, *Motherhood in the Old South*, 87–88.

7. For a discussion of the rising rate of confidence that antebellum women invested in male physicians, see McMillen, *Motherhood in the Old South*, 4–9, 74. She concludes, "It is doubtful that the doctors deserved such trust." Her research also reveals that it was not at all uncommon for a doctor to "serve at the accouchement of his own wife." McMillen, *Motherhood in the Old South*, 62.

You must excuse this short letter, and I will write more the next time. You must write soon and often, for I am very uneasy about you. The children all send there love to you, and you know that I do send all the love that a wife could send a kind and loveing husband. Oh, but I could see you this evening what a pleasure it would be to me. Give my love to Thomas.

I remain your wife as ever,
Emily A. M. Moxley

~

[*William M. Moxley to Emily Beck Moxley*]
Camp Memmenger
Febry. 14th, 1862
E. A. M. Moxley

My dear Emily,

I have been greatly disappointed to night, for I expected to recive a letter from you, but I fear the reason is because you are not able to write or I should have heard from you. I dont blame you, for I believe you will write to me when you can. You dont know how uneasy I am about you. I do not sleep as well as I did 2 months ago. I dreamed last night I went home & was there before I found I had no furlough. Then I had to get back as soon as posible. It is well I went home as soon as I did or I should not have seen you in a long time. They will not let any person have furloughs now that is able to fight Yankies.

You stated in your last letter to me to come home the last of this month. I would do so if I could, but it is imposible. But I earnestly hope the day will come when I can see home and evry thing that is dear to me again and my Country free. Then I will be happy as any man on earth, but while I am so distantly seperated from you and my children I cant be happy. It is out my power to be so. If happy at al, it is only for a few moments.

I want you to come when you get able if we should still remain here, which I recon we will, for the Government is doing a bundance of work at this place. I want you to come. If I can only get to see you once a week I should consider myself well paid. I think you can get some person to stay with Hannah an the children untill you can come and stay one month.

If I should get sick, I should want you for a nurse, but I hope I will remain healthy, for my health is very good at this time and has been so ever since I left you. Thomas & Newton are both well. My company is in better health than it has been since I left I left Auburn. Evrry thing is going on verry well.

Our Regiment is well armed and has amunition aplenty & well prepared to give the Yankies a warm reception. It is believd we will have a fight before long. If so I hope it may be the closing fight, for I am anxious to see the end of this war. I think it must close by next fall at furthest, but if I know it would close even that soon I would be better satisfied. 2 Regiments from our Brigade has been orderd to Tennessee. They will leave in the morning. They will have a cold time, for it has turned cold since 12 Oclock to day very fast. My hand is cold at this time.

You can tell Mr. Stringer and M. B. Stinson the Boys are well.[8] Curtis's Company is in better health now than it has been for several months. I dont [know] whether Newton will succeed in geting his commission or not. There was an Act passed Congress the 11th day of December last entilling all such offices to be filled by promotion. If it applies to his case he will not succeed. If he dont, it will be a bad chance for the Company to fill up, for there are but few persons that will goin the Company in its present condition.

There was a fight in Tennessee yesterday. Our men repulsed the Yankies 3 times. They left of [f] fireing and with drew their Troops, but was expected to renew the attact this morning. I have not heard whether it was the case or not.

You tell John Stringer if him & Green dont send their papers back soon it will be too late, if not already the case. They hate to give up verry. I should regret verry much if the matter should fail now after so much has been done.

I must close as I have nothing more of importance to write that would interest you. Give my best wishes to your Pa & Ma & the family. Kiss little Davis for me, & tell all the other children I think of them often and want to see them all bad enough. Tell them to be good children for my sake. Tell Hannah her brothers are both well. I have

8. Wilson B. Stringer's sons James M. and John B. were in Company B of the Twenty-fifth Alabama with the Beck brothers, as were Elias Green Stinson and Micajah Jason Stinson, the company's sergeant. At the beginning of February 1862, the Eighteenth and the Twenty-fifth Alabama regiments were stationed near each other outside Mobile.

not got into my house yet but I think will by to morrow night. I wish I knew more to write for it is my greatest pleasure. It is the only thing comes any ways near to conversing with the objects of our affections. Give my respects to Hannah & enquiring friends.

Your most devoted Husband
W. M. Moxley

~

[*Emily Beck Moxley to William M. Moxley*]
Pike Co., Ala.
Feb. 16, 1862
W. M. Moxley

Dear Husband,

I again take my seat to write you a few lines, though you may never get it, but I will try and fullfill my promise in writing. I have not got but one from you since you left, and that was wrote the 3 of this month. I am very uneasy about you. I heard last Friday that they were fighting in Pensacola and that 3 regiments had gone there from Mobile.[9] If that be true, I believe the 18th is one of them and I cant hear from you.

I saw D. Justice last Tuesday. He gave me 17.50 cts. in gold that his Brother brought from you to me. He [said] you had sent a trunk to me and he had left it in Greenville at [*name illegible*] Johnson's at the Livery stables. He sent me the key to the trunk, but I dont know when I will get the trunk. I am afraid it will be opened before I get it. I want you to write to me and let me know what you sent in it, and if you sent any thing to any body els I want to know the price of it and how much.

Sunday night at home I wrote the above. At Pa's to day, and since I heard that Mr. Oatis[10] was going to Greenville in the morning, and I thought I would send this by him.

We are all well to night and I hope this may find you the same. My Dear Husband, I do hope you will come home in a week from this

9. This report was not true, and in fact, Confederate forces were at that time evacuating the Pensacola area to reinforce Albert Sidney Johnston's army at Corinth.

10. This is most likely Nathaniel G. Oattis, who was listed as a twenty-four-year-old teacher at Court Schools in the 1860 Pike County census.

time for I am very anxious for you to come. It would give me more satisfaction than any thing, but I am afraid you will never see this, for you may be at Pensacola, and if so, perhaps you are dead. But, Oh, my Dear Husband, I do hope and pray that you are not. Oh, the uneasy hours I do spend now. My Dear, this is the third letter that I have wrote to you since you left and have not got but one from my Dear Husband. Dont you know I am miserable? You must write often. I cant think of any thing to write that will interest you, for all I do study about is my Husband that is far away from me.

Hanah says, tell her brothers, both of them, that they must write to her, and for them to direct theire letters to New Providence, and that she has not heard from home since William left, nor from them, and she is very anxious to hear from them. She is in trouble as well as I am, but there is nothing but trouble in this world for us to see, or it seems so to me, but I hope the day will come when we can enjoy our selves together.

My Dear, do try and be prepard to meet Death at any time, for we know not when [or] how soon it may come. Remember this if you never get another letter from me, for it is frome one that loves you well.

I must close. The children send there love to you and receive all that pen and ink can put down from me.

> Yours
> E. A. Moxley

~

[*Jourdan Beck to William M. Moxley*]
Feby 16th 1862
Capt. W. M. Moxley

Dear Son, as Emily is writing to you, I thought I would drop you a few lines, which leaves myself & family all tolerably well. Allen is still improving finely. He has been riding about the settlement a little. Jack Shaw's wife died the next Monday night after you left here, she was taken with flooding on Sunday night about 12 Oclock & died a little after dark the next night, without being delivered. She liked about 2 weeks of going her time out. Mitchel is up & a bout. Baker Stinson was sick the other day but is better. Mrs. Jackson had a negro boy to get his thigh broke yesterday evening. Louisa Stinson is improving finely. She was over at W. B. Stringer's the other day. I believe the balance of our neighbors are well except A. Shaw's wife.[11] She is very poorley yet.

Jason Stinson is going to take a school at Union Acadamy, to commence in the morning.

We have had a good deal of rain since you left here. Waters are high.

Well, Capt., I have hunted deligently for them hogs, but cant find but the one you saw. I killed him last week. I think some person has killed the other 3 & 2 sows that belonged to [Charles A.] T[hompson Beck] & a hog that Mat bought from A. Shaw that went with T's hogs. The six hogs, I think, would have made over 1000 lbs. of pork.

Some of us feels badly disappointed. Time will prove the thing; I believe it will prove true. I can[t] find the shoats that went with the hogs. Emily & Mat is both left in a bad fix a bout meat unless we can find them, which I doubt verry much. Suspicion rests some where.

There has not any waggon been to Greeneville from this settlement since you left. We had no mail last Monday; we are without any news of importance. We have understood that they commenced fighting at Pensicola last Wednesday & that 3 Regiments was sent there from Mobile, but we did not learn what Regiments they were.

I want you to write me what kind of a showing I must send to you, so that you can get what is coming to T & send it to me. Burt [Robertus W. Reeves] sent T's trunk, & I found in it a pr of pants & shirt & a coat & a pr of No 10 shoes. The coat & pants, I think, is large enough for J. Caldwell.[12] I wish he had let the officers that bought them keep them. I am not willing to pay a cent for them if I can keep from it. Had I not better send them back? Burt did not write to me who they were for.

Give my respects to D. N[ewton] M[oxley] & Thomas M[oxley] & R. W. R[eaves] & J[ames] M. S[tringer] & all the boys & S[amuel] J. P[ollard], & receive a good portion to yourself. Betsey sends her best respects to you & the rest of the boys. So I must close. Write soon.

> I remain yours as ever & c.
> Jourdan Beck &
> Elizabeth Beck
> To Capt. W. M. Moxley

---

11. Alexander Shaw, a near neighbor of the Moxleys, was married to Martha Shaw, age fifty-four. The couple had an eighteen-year-old son, William H. Shaw.

12. John Caldwell, age forty-six, owned a farm near that of the Becks.

~

[*William M. Moxley to Emily Beck Moxley*]
Camp Meminger
Febry. 21st, 1862
E. A. M. Moxley

My dear Emily,

I am again writing to you without hearing one word from since the 3rd day of this month. You may judge how uneasy I am, knowing it is not your fault. I am not displeased with you, but I would freely give 5 dollars to hear from you to night. But no chance. I do hope to hear from you soon. Lt. McDougald[13] is going to start home in the morning, but he will have to go by Montgomry in consequence of the Rail Road being washed up. He will take this letter to New Providence, & I hope he will send it to you, for I know you cant [get] letters now in consequence of high water, for I dont know when it rained any more than has rained here in the last ten days, & I think it [will] rain again before morning, but I shall be better prepared to receive it than when I was in tents.

I now have a room 14 feet by 12 finished off with a good stove, but I dont know how long the Yankies will [allow] me to enjoy it, for our officers say they are looking for this place to be attacked soon. I hope we will be more successful than our men was in Tennessee, but they did good fighting. Genl Piller[14] says that our men's guns was bloody from the point of the Bayonet to the Breach. The present is a dark hour, but I hope the dawn of a better day is not far off. I have heard so much bad news & bad weather lately & [am] so uneasy about you I can neither eat nor sleep much, though my health is good yet.

I have Headache some more than I did before I went home. My Company is in good health, none but what is able to be up. Newton's

---

13. H. H. McDugald was the first lieutenant of Company B, Twenty-fifth Alabama Infantry, until his resignation on 26 June 1862.

14. Brig. Gen. Gideon Johnson Pillow of Tennessee was second in command to Brig. Gen. John B. Floyd at Fort Donelson and led the abortive breakthrough attempt on 15 February 1862 to escape Grant's siege lines. Initially successful, Pillow lost his nerve and yielded the initiative, dooming the garrison to surrender. Pillow, himself, however, turned over command of the fort—Floyd having previously fled—to Simon Bolivar Buckner and made good his escape. His service thereafter was mercifully minimal. Hughes and Stonesifer, *The Life and Wars of Gideon J. Pillow*.

case is still in doubt. I dont know what they will do. The Company is anxious to have him for their Capt., & I wish they could. I cant write you a long letter this time, for I have nothing to write that would interest you but war news, and you will get it before this letter reaches you.

I expect to send some rice as soon as they get done with repairing the R. Rail so I can ship it to Greenville without going to Mont-gom[e]ry. If you need any thing, you must let me know it.

I cant go to Mobile as often as I could some time since. All men on Furloughs has been ordered back to camps. The only chance McDougall could get off was in concequence of his Company being below the standard, [and] he was sent home to Recruit it, but I dont believe he can get many under the circumstances.

I saw an order from Head Quarters the other day to discharge the Boys. I was glad enough, for they did evry thing they could to prevent it. I know some of them was greatly disappointed.

Some think we will be sent to Tennessee before long, but I dont think so, for they have already sent from here 3 Regiments, & they will not send us off unless they intend to leave Mobile to the Yankies to take. But if we do go away from here, we will have to go by Green-ville, so I intend to go home if I dont stay but one day.

But I hope you will be able to come down here before we leave. I want you to see this place, for it would be a considerable sight to you.

Well, now I must close my letter to you and dream of you the balanc of the night as I have done repeatedly since I left home. I never have been so uneasy in my life. I would not remain so long for nothing chould be given me. You know how I am when distressed in mind. It almost makes me sick. It distroys my appetite com-pleetly.

Tell Hannah her brothers are well. I will finish this letter to the children in the morning. Tell your Pa I would write to him this time if I could, but I shant have time. I was in charge of a working party of eighty men to day and did not have time untill to night. Give my best wishes to all my Relativs & Friends.

Your Effectionate Husband,
W. M. Moxley

⁓

[*William M. Moxley to His Children*]
Feb. 22d[, 1862]
George, Betty, Laura, & Willie

Dear Children,

How are you this Saturday morning? I hope you are all well. Have you all been good children since Pa left you? Have you minded Ma? George, my son, do you take care of your Sisters & Brothers? George, be a good boy. Mind your Ma & take care of little Davis. Ma, kiss him for me.

Goodby, Children.
W. M. Moxley

⁓

[*Emily Beck Moxley to William M. Moxley*]
Pike Co., Ala.
Feb. 24, 1862
W. M. Moxley

My Dear Husband,

I again take my seat to write you a few lines. This leaves us all well as common in body but not in mind. I received your kind letter Saturday evening which [you] wrote the 7 of this month. It was old, but I was glad to get it. I do hope I may get an othere to morrow. The river is so high that no person has crossed it untill there, and they had to cross in a batto [i.e., *bateau*]. The slew bridges are gone.

My Dear Husban, I am in a great deal of trouble about you. I heard this morning that Hariet Dillard got a letter from camps which stated that you had been put under Gard and punished in some way and turned out of office, but I hope that this is not so. I live in hope if I die in despare. Do write to me soon and write all about it, for I am so anxious to hear the strait of it. I have expected that they would punish you for what you have done for the boys if they could, and the General will allways have a spite at you for what others have told him about you. I have dreaded this all the time. You know I told you when you was here that I was uneasy about you, and now I am more so.

Oh, but I could hear from you this morning how much satisfaction it would give me. Nothing but your company would give me more, but I do hope and pray that you are well and doing well, so far as could be expected.

Well, my Dear Husband, you wrote you had sent me some things. I have not got them yet nor I dont know when I will, but that does not trouble me in the least, but I think I will get them in a week if it does not rain any more.

I heard yesterday that the Yankes had taken Savanah,[15] but I hope it is not so. But they are gaining ground very fast now from what we hear. It seams that God has forsaken us. I think if the officers of the present day were such men as the old revolutioners were, we would be more successfull in our battles that are fought. But the officers are in for money and do not think of the responsibility that rests upon there heads. They ought not to go for money alone. If they go to defend there country, let them go with a pure motive and with a heart that can feel for there men that are under them and treat them as brothers, for they are, in one sence of the word, for they are all enlisted for the same perpose, or ought to be, at least.

God grant that we may gain the victory and all can go home to their familiys and live in peace and comfort, for there are many distressed families in our country now, and I fear will there will be many more before peace is made. We think we see trouble now, which we do, but we do not know yet what we may have to contend with, but I believe if the people were to do as they should in such times as these that God would be with them unto the end, but who will do this?

I have some good news to write. Pa has found my hogs. After the river got up, they came out to there old range and he found [them] and he has them in a pen at his house. They look very well. Caldwell has killed Mat's, but he says he will pay Mat for him.

I am at Pa's now. They are all well as common. Pa and Allen is gone out to Henderson's[16] to day. I have started Betty to school. I have not sent George any yet. I cannot do with out him yet, for I want him to attend to Little Davis and cut wood and make fires.

15. Savannah, Georgia, one of the South's last remaining ports, remained in Confederate hands until 21 December 1864, when it fell to William T. Sherman's marauding army.

16. The hamlet of Henderson, Alabama, was three miles from the Beck home. The store there was owned and operated by Jeremiah A. Henderson, a thirty-year-old merchant, and his wife, Milley E. Henderson, twenty-five. Willis D. Henderson, twenty-four, a partner in the store, lived with his brother and sister-in-law.

Monday evening,

Dear Husband, since writing the above I have heard that Nashville, Tenn., has been taken by the Yankes. They are gaining the day fast. I see no chance for us now, or but very little, at least. I am expecting every day to hear that Mobile is taken and you all killed or taken prisoners. Oh, what will become of us then? We will have to come under the Northern Goverement. That will be awfull for us to do, to have to submit after looseing all that is near and dear to us in this world, but I fear we will have it to do.

I shall have to close. This is four letters that I have wrote to you and have not got but two from you, but I hope I will hear from you in the morning. I do wish you could be here this week. It would be a great satisfaction to me. The children all send their love to you, and you must receive a good portion from me.

So farewell for this time.
E. A. M. Moxley

~

[*Jourdan Beck to William M. Moxley*]
After 4 Oclock P.M.
Feby. 24th/62
Capt. W. M. Moxley

Dear Son,

As Emily is done writing, I will write a few lines wich leaves me & family all well. Emily seems disheartened, but my faith is not gone yet. I hope the day is not far distant when we will be able to drive the Yankeys back. I have been expecting some reverces; it would be to[o] good to fight them 12 months & never get whipt. The report a bout taking Savannah, I think is a mistake. It is a place in Tenasee by that name that our folks burnt & left it.[17] I cant say about Nashville; that may be true, but I hope not.

Mr. [Nathaniel G.] Oat[t]is is trying to make up an independent

---

17. On 5 March 1862, Federal major general C. F. Smith occupied Savannah, Tennessee, northeast of Corinth, Mississippi, where Albert Sidney Johnston was concentrating the Army of Tennessee in an attempt to resist the further advance of Union forces under U. S. Grant and Don Carlos Buell. There, Grant established his headquarters, and there he was when the battle of Shiloh commenced a few miles to the south on 6 April 1862.

company in Pike. He is now gone to Montgomery to try to make some arangements about it. I am told there is a call for 400 more volunteers from this county. If they dont volunteer they say they will have to draft them. Mat speaks of going with Oatis, but I cant say what he will do yet. Apple[ton] sayes he is going with him.

The [Conecuh] river has been about one foot & a half higher than it has been since I have been here. Smiley's[18] bridge is gone, & Ellis'es so I am told.

Allen is improving very fast lately. I have not time to write much at this time. We are all very anxious to hear from you all. I expect we will get some news to morrow. There is no chance to ride to the [post] office. For that reason I cant go this evening, for it would be dark coming home. So receive our best respects to you & the rest of the boys. So fare well for the present.

I remain yours as ever & c.
Jourdan Beck

~

[*Allen D. Beck to William M. Moxley*]
Pike Co., Ala.
Feb. 25th, 1862
W. M. Moxley

Dear Brother,

I now take my pen in hand to write you a few lines to let you know that we are all well. I have fattened the most you ever saw, but I am weak yet.

Dock, I heard you were under guard and that you were about to be turned out of office. I *suppose* Col. Lumis says that we boys shall not draw any money, but I believe my part of that.

Breakfast is ready and I must close. You must write to us often.

I have not got into any business yet. Mat is talking of taking a school at Bullock again this year, and not charge the patron any thing at all, just have what the Co[unty] pays. So I will quit for this time.

A. D. Beck

18. Stephen D. and Mary M. Smilie owned a sizable farm on the Conecuh River near the Beck home.

6

"*As well as common*"

28 February 1862–2 April 1862

The crisis for the Confederacy that was created by U.S. Grant's successful invasion of Tennessee in the winter of 1861–1862 broke up the garrison at Mobile and, ironically, fulfilled Leroy P. Walker's desire by forcing its reassignment to Albert Sidney Johnston's army, now pushed back into northeast Mississippi. On 26 February 1862, Bragg ordered the Eighteenth, the Twenty-second Alabama, and Col. Daniel W. Adams's First Regular regiment of Louisiana infantry, to Corinth, Mississippi, "to receive further orders."[1]

There, with Col. John C. Moore's Second Texas Infantry, Col. Joseph Wheeler's Nineteenth Alabama, Lt. Col. Robert C. Farris's Seventeenth Alabama, and Capt. Isadore P. Girardey's Washington Light Artillery Battery, the Eighteenth became part of the new 2,208-man Third Brigade, Whithers's Division, [Bragg's] Second Corps, Army of Mississippi—to be commanded by Brig. Gen. John King Jackson of Georgia.[2]

1. Braxton Bragg to Judah P. Benjamin, 14 January 1862, *OR*, vol. 6, p. 806; Special Orders No. 62, Headquarters, Department of Alabama and West Florida, Mobile, Ala., 26 February 1862, *OR*, vol. 6, p. 836.
2. *OR*, vol. 10, pt. 1, p. 383.

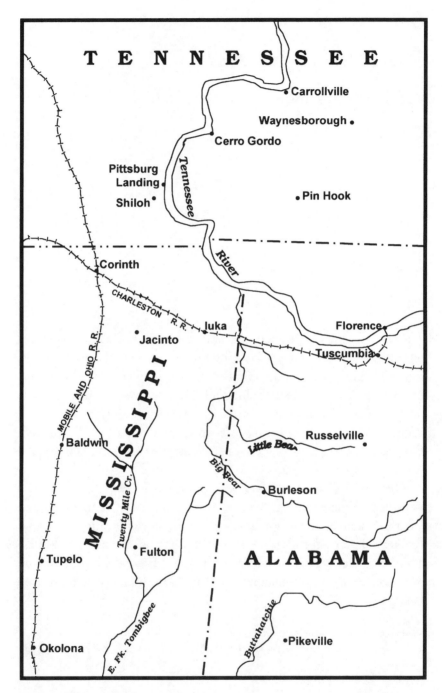

Figure 6. Theater of Operations of the Army of Tennessee, Spring and Summer 1862 (map by Susan Young)

After what Jackson described as "a fatiguing march and great exposure to bad weather," the brigade arrived at its rendezvous point near Pittsburgh Landing, Tennessee, at noon on Saturday, 5 April.[3] The Eighteenth, now commanded by Col. Eli S. Shorter, fought the first day at Shiloh, 6 April 1862, playing a conspicuous role in the capture of Brig. Gen. Benjamin Mayberry Prentiss's division in the Hornet's Nest. As evidence of the severity of the Eighteenth Alabama's action, Shorter reported that within an hour and a half of fighting, every man of the regiment fired off the fifty rounds of cartridges that they had carried into battle. Of the 413 noncommissioned officers and privates engaged, 20 were killed and 80 wounded. The casualties included the regiment's lieutenant colonel, James Thadeus Holtzclaw, who "received a terrific shot through the body" and had to be borne on a litter twenty miles back to Corinth. Colonel Shorter reported Holtzclaw "dangerously wounded" early in the battle "while he was gallantly discharging his duty," and Pvt. Edgar W. Jones later wrote, "The only field officers who impressed me that day by their gallantry were Maj. [sic] Holtzclaw and Col. Joe Wheeler."[4]

"Most of those classed among the missing," Shorter reported, "doubtless were taken prisoners by the enemy, as they were with Dr. Barnett, our surgeon, who was captured on Monday while attending to the wounded. It is reported to me on good authority that the enemy fired on Dr. Barnett and his party while under the yellow flag and when the surgeon was actually engaged in dressing the wounds of one of the enemy." The officers and men of the regiment, wrote Shorter, "conducted themselves throughout the several engagements with much gallantry and spirit." Only one officer, Lt. E. J. Rogers, who was in command of Company B, disgraced himself, abandoning his company twice and wholly disappearing before the fight was finished.[5]

On 7 April the Eighteenth Alabama was detailed to escort the captured division back to Corinth and so missed the second day's fighting.

3. John King Jackson, Corinth, Miss., 26 April 1862, OR, vol. 10, pt. 1, pp. 553–556.

4. Eli S. Shorter, at Corinth, to Capt. J. B. Cummings, Assistant Adjutant General, 9 April 1862, OR, vol. 10, pt. 1, p. 557. Jones, History of the 18th Alabama Infantry, n.p.

5. Eli S. Shorter, at Corinth, to Capt. J. B. Cummings, Assistant Adjutant General, 9 April 1862, OR, vol. 10, pt. 1, p. 557.

"Prentiss proved to be a most surly, crusty prisoner," Private Jones remembered, "cursing everything in sight, even to the soil of the country; snarling and snapping at everything."[6]

William M. Moxley had become the Eighteenth Alabama's second major with James Thadeus Holtzclaw's promotion to lieutenant colonel in December 1861. He retained this rank, although apparently absent from the army much of the time, until his resignation on 21 April 1862. Moxley was replaced by Sheppard Ruffin. In his memoir of service with the Eighteenth Alabama, Pvt. Edgar W. Jones recalled that J. M. McLaughlin of Company C was promoted to major after Ruffin's death during the Atlanta campaign, but official records indicate that Bryan Morel Thomas became the regiment's fourth and final major.[7]

[*D. Newton Moxley to Emily Beck Moxley*]
Mobile, Ala.
Feb. 28, 1862
Mrs. E. Moxley

Dear Sistor,

By the request of Brother, I seat my self to in forme you that he left hear last night with a short notis for Corinth, Miss. Two regiments left, Col. Shorter's & Days's.[8] He was well. All so Brother Thomas.

6. The standard treatments of the battle of Shiloh are Daniel, *Shiloh;* McDonough, *Shiloh;* and Sword, *Shiloh.*

7. Muster of Field and Staff Officers, 13 June 62, Eighteenth Alabama Infantry, Alabama Department of Archives and History; *List of Field Officers, Regiments and Battalions in the Confederate States Army, 1861–1865,* 88; Jones, *History of the 18th Alabama Infantry.*

8. Zachariah Cantey Deas, a Mobile cotton broker and Mexican War veteran, served briefly as Albert Sidney Johnston's aide-de-camp at the beginning of the war and then raised, financed, and was elected to the command of the Twenty-second Alabama Infantry, which was organized at Montgomery on 6 October 1861. Two of the regiment's companies—I, commanded by Capt. Andrew P. Love, and K, commanded by Capt. Benjamin R. Hart—were raised in Pike County. Like the Eighteenth Alabama, the Twenty-second was posted at Mobile during the winter of 1861 and was then ordered to Corinth as part of Adley Hogan Gladden's brigade. When Gladden was wounded in the first day's fighting at Shiloh, Deas took command of his brigade until he, too, was wounded the following day. Deas was promoted to brigadier general on 13 December 1862. He and the Twenty-second took part in Bragg's Kentucky campaign, fought at Murfreesboro, at Chickamauga, and at the siege of Chattanooga. The regiment took part in the Atlanta campaign as part of George D. Johnston's brigade and in John Bell Hood's Tennessee campaign. During the final days of the war the Twenty-second was consolidated with the Twenty-fifth, the Thirty-ninth,

I am hear in Mobile, sick. I have [been] sick for severl days, ever since the tornado we had the other night. I cant give you a description of it now, but the like has never bin sean. My tent was blown away, & I still tryed to hold to my bunk and did so till I was blown off. We got a good many cripled. The large two story hospital blowne over & did kill only one nurse ded. A grat manny treeas blew down on tentes & cripled a grat manny [*phrase illegible*] of over. Sum got wounded but not seaverley crippled. James Stringer was in the tent with me & was blown off when the tent blew down.[9]

Willson Stinson was quit[e] sick with mumpes when I left Campes.

You must say to those boys that they must com back, as thar Dis Charges was not leagle. William toled me to say to you to tell them to com soon. They are advertised as Desserters. The reason why their papers would not stand was in concequence of Curtis having his resignation in three days be fore he sind thar papers.

I must close. I will writ again soon. You must excuse this as it is don in the grates hurry.

Yours,

D. N. Moxley

⁓

[*Emily Beck Moxley to D. Newton Moxley*]
Pike Co., Ala.
March 10, 1862
D. N. Moxley

Dear Brother,

I seat my self to write you a few lines. These lines leaves us all well as common, and I hope they find you in better health than you was when you wrote to me.

---

and the Twenty-sixth–Fiftieth under Col. Harry Theophilus Toulmin but surrendered only days later at Greensboro, North Carolina.

9. "One night about midnight there came upon us a most fearful and terrific cyclone accompanied by an awful downpour of rain," recalled Pvt. Edgar W. Jones. "We were all in comfortable plank cabins, most of which were unroofed and many blown down. The hospital, containing thirty-six men, was blown flat to the ground. It was remarkable that but one man was killed, and he was the sentinel at the door. It was pitiful and distressing to hear the cries and groans of the men under the wreck. Many men in the quarters were wounded. One afterwards died. It was a most thrilling experience." Jones, *History of the 18ᵗʰ Alabama Infantry.*

I received your kind letter last Saturday morning, which I was very glad to get but was sorry to hear that the Dr. was gone to Miss., but he will have to go where ever they please to send him, for he is under the controll of the Government and will have to obey the commands that are given him. I am sorry that you could not go with him, for I know it would have been a satisfaction to him, and I would be better satisfied to know that you and him were together, but that is not as we please.

I heard yesterday that Colonel Lumis Regiment had left Mobile, but did not hear where they were. Some said they had gone to Miss., some said to Tennessee. The boys are going to start back in a few days. They dont know yet where they will have to go to. They will go with Lt. McDougle. He is here at this time.

I shall send this letter by Allen to you, but you never stated whether you was Capt. of that Company or not, but I heard that you was. I allso heard that the Dr. was Major of Shorter's Regiment. I do not know that is so. I want you to write to me and give me the latest news from the Dr. as I am very uneasy about him. I expect you can hear from him sooner that I can. He stated in his last letter to me that he had not heard from home since the 3 day of last month, but I have wrote several letters to him since that time. If he did not get them, you must write to him and let him know that we are all well. I shall send a letter to Corrinth, Miss., but I dont know when he will get it.

The health of the neighborhood is good, so far as I know. [Joseph] Franklin Stinson's child is dead. That is all the death we have had lately, that I have heard of.

Mr. John Stinson wants to know what the Dr. done with Lafaett's and Robbert's affairs. He says he wants to know if he got their pay or what he done about it. If you know any thing about it, write and let him know.

I must close, for I have nothing to write that would interest you. Write soon.

Yours, as ever,
E. A. M. Moxley

Emily Moxley and her baby died on 13 March 1862 and were buried in the Spears Cemetery, Pike County, Alabama, beside her brother Charles A. Thompson Beck.

Her gravestone reads:

> Emily A. Moxley
> 13 March 1862
> Aged 25 years 11 months 26 days
> Wife of W. M. Moxley[10]

[*William M. Moxley to George E. Moxley*]
Corinth, Miss.
April 2nd, 1862
George E. Moxley

My dear Son,

I write you afew lines to let you know you have a Father who loves you dearly with your little Sisters & Brothers. George, I have often told you to be a good boy, mind your Mother, and take care of your Sisters & Brothers. George, I cant say so any more. Your dear Mother is gone now, George. Mind your Grand Pa & Ma and evry person that teaches you to do right. George, you are the eldest. As you have no Ma, always take care of your little Sisters & Brothers. Be good to them & be a good boy. If your Pa should die or get killed in Battle, then you would have niether Father nor Mother to advise you.

George, keep this paper; get it by heart. Your Grand Pa will read it for you. Besure to keep it untill I go to see you, & if I should die, keep it untill you are a man. Read it to your sisters & Brothers.

George, be a good boy. Betty, you & Laura be good children. Mind when told. Take care of little Willie & Thomson. You are all dear children to me. Your Pa loves you dearly & will do all he can for you. I do hope to see you before a great while.

> Good by, my dear children.
> Your loving Father,
> W. M. Moxley

10. Although no record of the cause of her death exists, one may safely assume that Emily Moxley succumbed to one of the several horrors that stalked the nineteenth-century birthing chamber: hemorrhaging, puerperal convulsions, prolonged labor, placenta previa, or sepsis, the single largest cause of maternal death, for as Sally G. McMillen points out, "few doctors took the precaution of cleaning either their instruments or their hands." McMillen, *Motherhood in the Old South*, 95–97.

Maj. William M. Moxley resigned from the army at Tupelo, Mississippi, on 21 April 1862 and returned to Bullock. Although he accompanied his regiment to Corinth as its newly promoted major, he was apparently not present for duty at the battle of Shiloh. In 1862 Moxley was approximately forty-eight years of age, well advanced by the standard of Civil War leadership characterized by "boy generals" in their early twenties, and Pvt. Edgar W. Jones of Company G observed that a number of the regiment's officers were "men well advanced in years." Moxley and captains James T. Brady of Company B, James Haughey of Company G, and Guy Smith and Charles M. Cox of Company D he all judged to be over fifty years of age, and four of these officers, as well as captains James M. Oliver of Company C, Henry Clay Armstrong of Company F, and John J. Calhoun of Company K, left the regiment early in the war. Haughey, Jones recalled, "served through Shiloh," implying that Moxley did not, and mention of his presence is conspicuously absent from Colonel Shorter's report on the battle. "These old men could not stand the fatigue and exposure of camp life and soon thinned out."

Moxley submitted his resignation on 21 April 1862 and left the regiment at Tupelo, Mississippi. "After the battle of Shiloh," Jones reported, "the regiment was without field officers and was for a short time under officers detailed for the purpose."[11]

The *Southern Advertiser* of 28 January 1863 noticed that Moxley's Coffee County property was "to be sold for taxes at Elba" on the fourth Monday in March 1863. At Bon Secour, Alabama, Moxley went into the mercantile business, selling groceries, dry goods, and notions. His 1863 account book lists quantities of bacon, hams, pickled pork, chickens, corn, rice, peas, salt, pepper, sugar, and molasses as well as tobacco, lumber, nails, rope, kettles, whiskey, envelopes, shoes, needles, thread, and buttons that had been produced locally or had run the blockade at Mobile.

11. *List of Field Officers, Regiments and Battalions in the Confederate States Army, 1861–1865,* 88.

7

"It really seems that we have worse luck than any other set of men in the known world"

3 May 1862–17 December 1864

Disaster followed disaster, with the lost opportunity at Shiloh on 6–7 April and the fall of New Orleans on 25 April. By the beginning of May, the South had lost 100,000 square miles of its territory—including 1,000 miles of navigable rivers—and the value of the Confederate dollar had fallen to even lower depths.

After retreating from Shiloh, the Eighteenth rejoined the Army of Tennessee, now commanded by Gen. Pierre Gustave Toutant Beauregard, at Corinth, Mississippi. There it awaited the further movements of the combined forces of U.S. Grant and Don Carlos Buell, now under the direct supervision of Maj. Gen. Henry Halleck. After a ponderous advance of fifteen miles that took six weeks, Halleck at last forced the Confederates out of Corinth on 29 May 1862.[1] From there, Beauregard's army marched twenty miles to Clear Creek, where it remained for four days before falling back on Tupelo and then Saltillo, Mississippi. As

---

1. Halleck's otherwise unaccountable tardiness in following Beauregard's badly mauled army may be explained by the prevalence of disease in the Union army. By the time Halleck occupied Corinth, a third or more of his men had fallen ill, and in July 1862 more than half of his men and more than one-third of Beauregard's were on the sick list. During the Corinth campaign nearly half of the twenty-nine Union generals were stricken with malaria, dysentery, or some other disease common to camp life. Halleck himself was down with diarrhea, ruefully called "the evacuation of Corinth."

William Moxley's brother Benjamin Thomas Moxley wrote on 24 June, "this [w]hole Regt. has bin torned all to pieces since the battle of Shilo."

The Eighteenth Alabama remained stationed near Saltillo until 23 July 1862, when Maj. Gen. William J. Hardee, who took command of the Second Corps when Bragg replaced Beauregard as army commander, detached the Seventeenth and Eighteenth Alabama and the Eighteenth and Nineteenth Louisiana to garrison the fortifications at Mobile.[2]

There, under the successive commands of Brig. Gen. James Edwin Slaughter and Brig. Gen. Alfred Cumming, the Eighteenth remained until April 1863, when it rejoined the Army of Tennessee in a brigade with the Thirty-sixth and Thirty-eighth Alabama regiments and the Ninth Alabama battalion (later consolidated with the Thirty-second Alabama as the Fifty-eighth Alabama Infantry).

On 31 July 1863 the Eighteenth was attached to Henry DeLamar Clayton's brigade, Lt. Gen. Daniel Harvey Hill's corps. Clayton was succeeded in command of the brigade by James Thadeus Holtzclaw and then by Col. Bushrod Jones of Perry, Alabama.

At Chickamauga, 19–20 September 1863, the Eighteenth lost 22 of its 36 officers, and 300 of its 527 men, killed and wounded, 56 percent of those engaged. The Eighteenth's casualties at Chickamauga included the regiment's colonel, James Thadeus Holtzclaw, whose horse struck a tree.[3] The command of the regiment then devolved on Lt. Col. Richard Freer Inge of Tuscaloosa County. Inge had served as the first captain of the Confederate Stars, Company E, Eighteenth Alabama, but was promoted to lieutenant colonel when the regiment was organized at Auburn. Shortly after assuming command of the regiment, Inge was shot through the knee. Although the wound need not have been fatal, he died a week later, 28 September 1863. Pvt. Edgar W. Jones of Company G described Inge as "a brave, generous, kind-hearted man, and as an officer who sought to do his full duty to his men and his country. He was greatly loved by the men and officers, and his death was greatly

---

2. Special Orders No. 6, Tupelo, Miss., 23 July 1862, *OR*, vol. 16, pt. 2, p. 733.

3. Although Joseph Wheeler reported that Holtzclaw remained on the field, Pvt. Edgar W. Jones recalled seeing an unspecified field-grade officer—but clearly the colonel—"turning up a bottle which I supposed contained whiskey, and I further thought he was trying to steady his nerve. I was not surprised when I learned afterward that his horse had fallen with him and disabled him to such an extent that he had to go to the rear."

deplored by the entire regiment." His name was inscribed on the Confederate Roll of Honor for his "courage and devotion on the field of battle" at Chickamauga.[4]

At Chattanooga, the Eighteenth suffered 209 casualties, including 90 men captured in the rout from Missionary Ridge, 25 November 1863. There, too, the regiment's "Hardee Pattern" battle flag was captured.

Following the humiliation at Chattanooga, the Eighteenth Alabama was reduced to 275 effectives, and after wintering and recruiting at Dalton, Georgia, the regiment began the Atlanta campaign with 500 men. It was engaged in near constant skirmishing in the retreat to Jonesborough and lost very nearly half its number in the battles in and around Atlanta—Peachtree Creek, 20 July; Atlanta, 22 July; Jonesborough, 31 August–1 September; and Lovejoy's Station, 2–6 September.

With the fall of Atlanta, the Eighteenth accompanied Lt. Gen. John Bell Hood on his disastrous Tennessee campaign, losing about 100 men, principally captured, at Franklin, 20 November 1864. In February 1865, the regiment was ordered back to Mobile, where it became part of the garrison of Fort Blakely, Spanish Fort, Alabama. After the heroic defense of that vital stronghold, 26 March–8 April 1865, the regiment escaped when the position was evacuated. The Eighteenth Alabama laid down its arms at Meridian, Mississippi, on 4 May 1865, with the surrender of Lt. Gen. Richard Taylor's Department of East Louisiana, Mississippi, and Alabama.[5]

With the crisis created by the fall of Forts Henry and Donelson and the capture of Nashville, the state of Alabama authorized the organization of the Thirty-third Alabama Infantry at Pensacola, Florida, on 23 April 1862. The Moxleys' friend and neighbor Appleton H. Justice recruited the Covington and Coffee Grays, Company F of the Thirty-third Alabama Infantry, and on 11 March 1862, when the company was organized at Brandon's Store, Rose Hill, Alabama, he was elected its captain. His son-in-law, Dr. Sidney A. Warren—formerly a boarder in the Moxleys' home—was elected the company's second lieutenant. Soon, however, ill health forced Justice to resign and turn the command over to his first lieutenant, William N. Brandon of Covington County.

4. Jones, *History of the 18th Alabama Infantry Regiment;* Carroll, *The Confederate Roll of Honor,* 15.

5. Brewer, *Willis Brewer's Alabama,* 589–705 ("Brief Historical Sketches of Military Organizations Raised in Alabama During the Civil War"); *Clayton's (Holtzclaw's) Brigade, 1862–1865* (1997): n. p.; Wheeler, *Alabama,* 113–114.

Samuel Adams, the regiment's first colonel, was twice elected to the House of Representatives before the war but resigned with his state's secession to become a first lieutenant in the Ninth Alabama Infantry. In February 1862 he was promoted to colonel of the Thirty-third Alabama. He was wounded at Perryville, Kentucky, while commanding a brigade but returned in time to lead his regiment at Murfreesboro and at the battle of Kennesaw Mountain, where he was mortally wounded on 21 July 1864.

The Thirty-third Alabama served in virtually every battle of the Army of Tennessee from Perryville to Nashville but disbanded shortly before Gen. Joseph E. Johnston surrendered to William T. Sherman at Durham Station, North Carolina, on 26 April 1865.

[*Appleton H. Justice to Martha E. Justice Warren,*
with postscript from Sidney A. Warren]

Fort Barrancas, Fla.[6]
Saturday, May 3rd, 1862

Mrs. M. E. Warren,[7]

I received your business letter a few minutes ago and hasten to reply. As to the business matter between myself and Mr. Knots, pay him $10.°° more and wait until I come home. Dont let him have any more corn at all. Tell him he did not bring the cotton at the time he was to, no how, and that cotton is not worth anything at all now. Just pay him ten dollars more, and if he is not satisfied, tell him to wait until I come home and I will fix it all up.

I have been sick, but am up again and will be entirely well in a few days.

Write often.
Yours, & c.,
A. H. Justice

6. Barrancas Barracks, originally known as Fort San Carlos de Barrancas, was located at Tartar Point on Pensacola Bay, five miles southwest of Pensacola, Florida, and opposite Fort Pickens on Santa Rosa Island. It was in Federal hands by mid-December 1864.

7. Martha E. Justice was the daughter of Appleton H. and Susan M. Justice and the wife of Dr. Sidney A. Warren. In 1862 she would have been eighteen years old.

P.S. Your Pa hired me to write this letter. I am like you [*word illegible*].
I have not got time to write to you myself. Your Pa says tell your Ma
to let Tommie [Augustus B. Tommy] have all those papers in that box,
letters and all, as he has no further use for them.

S. A. Warren

~

[*Sidney A. Warren to Martha E. Justice Warren*]
June 2ⁿᵈ, 1862

Mr. Mullins[8] did not get off to day as he expected, and it is some
what doubtful whether he does to morrow or not. I will continue to
write until he does get off, if any thing transpires. I was mistaken
about the 18ᵗʰ Ala. being in one mile of us. I do not know where they
are, but suppose they are some where not far off from here.[9]

The remaining 5 companies of our Regt. came in this morning, all
safe without any encounter with the enemy.

I feel pretty dull and stupid this morning. I was put on as Officer of
the Guard last night after marching 16 miles, and our guard quarters
are out under a large oak, and I had to sleep, what sleeping I done,
again on the ground.

I forgot to state to you in my last letter that Joe Buckaloo went off
from here indebted to me three dollars. I want you to have it collected.
Also, George Johnson, one dollar.[10] I loaned it to them on the way
here to buy shoes, and I think they ought to pay it.

I have not drawn any money yet, but whenever I do I will send you
some, if I have an opportunity. All our company have come in but Ben
Lewis, Charles Malloy, and Alex Baine.[11] Lewis & Malloy, I think, are
safe and will come in to day.

I want you to write to Sis or some of them and let them know all
about me, as you can tell them all, and I have not time to write to any

8. William B. G. Mullins, a private in Company F, Thirty-third Alabama Infantry, was a thirty-
year-old Coffee County farmer in 1860.

9. The Eighteenth Alabama was, in fact, encamped near Tupelo at the time.

10. Josephus Bucklew and George Johnston of Company A, Eighteenth Alabama Infantry, were
on sick furlough in Coffee County in December 1861. Pay and Muster Roll, Eighteenth Alabama
Infantry, December 1861, Alabama Department of Archives and History.

11. Benjamin Y. Lewis of Bullock was the second corporal of Company F, Thirty-third Alabama
Infantry. John Alexander Baine and Charles Malloy—the same Charles Malloy who had harvested
William Moxley's corn the year before and refused to return a share—were privates.

one but you. You may direct your letters, if you write soon, to Baldwin instead of Ocolona.[12] I will let you know when we move.

June 3rd, 1862

Mr. Mullins has entirely failed to get a discharge and will not get off at all. The Brigade Surgeon says the loss of his toe is no cause for a discharge.

Mr. Underwood[13] will be discharged, though, I guess, and will get off in a few days, so I will send it by him. There is an order in Camps, though not read out yet, not to allow any one to write any thing about the movements of the Army here. Consequently, I cannot write anything by mail and will [*fragment missing*] you a full account now. [*Name illegible*] took dinner with me to day. His Regiment is 7 miles above here. He was sent down with a detachment of 50 men to pick up the Stragglers belonging to Bragg's army who were lost or strayed.[14] He is well and doing finely. Our Cavalry brought in 65 yankee prisoners yesterday.

Our boys have all got in now but Baine & Ben Lewis. Charles Malloy has just got in.

There is an effort being made by the Officers of our Reg^t to get back to Pollard.[15] I do not know how it will come out. I do not make any calculations on it now. They are all very anxious to get back. It would be a great advantage to the health of the Regiment. We havent more than 200 men reported for duty in the Regiment now, and if it

12. By June 1862, the Army of Tennessee was lying around Tupelo, Mississippi. Baldwin, Mississippi, is some thirty miles south of Corinth and twenty miles north of Tupelo, and Okolona, Mississippi, is thirty-five miles south of Baldwin and fifteen miles south of Tupelo. All three were located on the Mobile and Ohio railroad.

13. J. A. H. Underwood was a private in Company F, Thirty-third Alabama Infantry.

14. In consequence of his ill health—in addition to the president's displeasure with the general's presumed failure to take the opportunity to destroy Grant's army at Shiloh and his retreat from Halleck's overwhelming force at Corinth—Jefferson Davis removed Beauregard from command of the Army of Tennessee and replaced him with Braxton Bragg. Not until 17 June, however, was Bragg officially promoted. As of 3 June, he still commanded only one of the army's four corps.

15. Pollard, Alabama, is forty miles north of Pensacola and fifty miles east by northeast of Mobile and is located at the junction of the Mobile and Great Northern Rail Road and the Alabama and Florida Rail Road. The strategic town remained in Confederate hands until 20 March 1865 as a position from which Rebel troops supported the defenses of Mobile and kept the Federal garrison at Pensacola in check. The Thirty-third Alabama was not, in fact, reassigned to the Pensacola area but took part in Braxton Bragg's Kentucky campaign of 1862 and most of the remaining battles of the Army of Tennessee.

does not get better we will not have more than 100 in a week. My
health keeps going [*word illegible*] all the time.

We have just heard the Gen. Johns[t]on has just whipped the
Yankees at Richmond.[16] Our troops here need hearing something sure
like that very much. I think it will have a good effect if it is confirmed.

I will continue to write every day until Mr. Underwood gets of[f],
if it is a week and I have time.

S. A. W.

Sidney A. Warren died on 6 July 1862, scarcely a month after writing
this letter.

[*James M. Stringer to William M. Moxley*]
Camp near Tupelo, Mississippi
June 23rd, 1862
Maj. W. M. Moxley

Dear Sir,

Your favor of the 17th just came to hand day before yesterday
evening, and I this morning hasten to answer. I was much gratified
to hear of your safe arrival at home and that you found all well.

Dr., this leaves me in as good health as when you left, and I do
hope it my find you enjoying the greatest of blessings. I am forced to
record the death of our much estemed friend Franklin Stinson, which
I have been enivitably informed occured a few days since at Oaklona,
Miss.[17]

It really seems that we have worse luck than any other set of men in
the known world. I have concluded to take things as they come and
complain at nothing if I can possibly help it. I do hope we will have no
more bad luck while we remain in the Service, but it seems to me the
more we desire a change for the better, the farther it gits from it.

The rest of the boys from our side of the river are all well and

16. The battle of Fair Oaks or Seven Pines, 31 May–1 June 1862, was the first in a bloody series
of battles in which the Confederate army seized the initiative from the Army of the Potomac and
began to drive it away from the Confederate capital. Although this was a tactical victory for the
North, Johnston's assault so unnerved McClellan that he yielded the initiative to the Confederate
army and began his painful withdrawal down the Peninsula. Newton, *Joseph E. Johnston and the
Defense of Richmond.*

17. Joseph Franklin Stinson died at Okolona, Mississippi, on 7 June 1862—three months after
the death of his son.

getting along finely. We are still at the same place where you left us, but I have no idea how long we will stay or where we will go when we do leave. Some say one place and some another. If we are sent back into our own state, I would be pleased to have a visit from you at any time and hope to be able to pay you all a visit in a short time. I would like to be with you on the banks of old Conecuh one time more with a pocket full of Mussuls, as I think I could enjoy it first rate.

Dr., there is no news in Camps that is worth attention that is reliable. Still there is considerable excitement in relation to the termination of the war. So for my part, I hardly know what to think, but there are some steps being taken, in my opinion, one way or the other, and I am unable to say which that way is but hope and trust it is to terminate the war if it is in our favor.

I have heard nothing of the enemy's movements since you left. I suppose Clanton's Cavalry[18] are gone back to see what they are doing up about Corinth, and if they are not there, they are to keep going until they do find out something in relation to their position.

We have a tolerably hard time now drilling, as it is tremendous dry and dusty and our whole time is filled up with the exception of a few hours during the middle of the day. Rain is greatly needed in this section of country.[19]

Dr., I will quit for this time as Allen wants to write some, and paper is very scarce and hard to get.[20] Write soon and often, and believe me, as ever, your friend and well wisher,

J. M. Stringer

(P.S.) Excuse this kind of writing, as it is the best I can do at present.

18. James Holt Clanton was born in Columbia County, Georgia, but moved with his family to Alabama in 1835. Elected colonel of the First Alabama Cavalry in the fall of 1861, he took part in the battle of Shiloh and then returned to Alabama to recruit and organize two more regiments that, with the First, were to constitute Clanton's Cavalry Brigade. He was promoted to brigadier general on 16 November 1863. Clanton's brigade was active in the Atlanta campaign and was then assigned to the Department of Alabama, Mississippi, and East Louisiana.

19. An unusually wet spring in north Mississippi was followed by a disastrously dry summer in 1862. Men and horses suffered for want of water, and Henry W. Halleck's army was largely immobilized after Beauregard's evacuation of Corinth because of the falling level of the rivers and the consequent impossibility of transportation or supply by water. McPherson, *Battle Cry of Freedom*, 414–418, 512.

20. Stringer's complaint provides further evidence in support of Bell I. Wiley's observation that

~

[*Allen D. Beck to William M. Moxley*]
Camp near Tupelo, Miss.
June 23rd, 1862
W. M. Moxley

Dear Brother,

As James has not written up all his paper, I will write you a few lines to let you know how I am getting along. I have had better health the last two weeks than I have had in some time. There is a great deal of talk now about peace, but I am afraid they are just fixing for a new start. If we could get enough to eat here we could do very well, but we had to eat bread with three days last week without meat or grees. I thought one time that I never would beg for meat skin to eat or pot licker to make up bread with, but I would have done it last week if I could have got it by beggin. They have give us more meat this week than they give us last week.

I do truly hope that I will eat at home before two months longer. They are discharging soldiers here about as fast as they can. There was six discharged in your old company yesterday, so I heard. I am afraid we will be ordered to Chattanooga. That is one place I never want to see again.[21]

I had better close. You must write often & tell all the rest of the family to write. I will write again. Give my love to all the family. Receive a portion to your self. Think of me when you go a fishing & when you are eating them. I remain yours as ever,

A. D. Beck

"the declining fortunes of the Southern Confederacy may be strikingly traced in the degeneration of the stationery used by ordinary soldiers." Old wrapping paper, fly pages from books, and even the reverse side of wallpaper were commonly used by soldiers and their families. The scarcity of paper, combined with the South's dizzying rate of inflation, sent the cost of a single quire of paper to five dollars and "a bunch of envelopes" to three dollars at a time when a Rebel private earned but eleven dollars a month. Wiley, *The Life of Johnny Reb*, 196–198.

21. Although the regimental muster roll does not specify when or under what circumstances, Allen D. Beck died at Chattanooga.

~

[Benjamin Thomas Moxley to William M. Moxley]
Tupelo,
June the 24th, 1862

Dear Brother,

With pleasure I write you a few lines which leaves me not well at this. I received your letter last Sunday which found me with the headache, and I have had it ever since. I had a hot fever yesterday & I never was as uneasy a bout anything before, for there is no place hear for sick people. You know this yourself.

William, this [w]hole Regt. has bin torned all to pieces since the battle of Shilo. J. H. Justice is capt. of Co. (A) and J. M. Harper is 2nd Liut of Co. (C) & Liut. Walker [22] from Co. F is our first Liut., & Capt. Starke trid to resin. He sent up his resignation & it was refuse by General Brag[g].

You stated in your letter about fishing. When you write to me, put that part out or where I can not hear of it, for it does me harm unless I could enjoy some of it, for there's no chance of enjoying any thing to eat hear, for you will have be smart to win your own rashion, & the only way I have found to have mine yet is to keep it around my neck and not eat any of it myself.

Moses Vann [23] return to the company the day after you left. He said that he would have bin glad to have seen you before you left, but he is Discharged though now & has gon home. He started last Sunday & Allen Priggen [24] to[o], & they are discharging the Soldiers now very fast at this time.

June the 25: I feel better this morning then I did yesterday. Enoch Ray is dead. [25]

22. This is apparently H. P. Walker of Jefferson County, who, upon the resignation of James Haughey on 27 May 1862, became captain of Company G, Eighteenth Alabama.

23. Moses Vann, Company A, Eighteenth Alabama, was detached from his company as a nurse for at least the months of November 1861 through January 1862. Hospital Pay and Muster Roll, Eighteenth Alabama Infantry, 31 October 1862, Alabama Department of Archives and History.

24. Allen Pridgen, Company A, Eighteenth Alabama, was on sick furlough in December 1861. Pay and Muster Roll, Eighteenth Alabama Infantry, December 1861, Alabama Department of Archives and History.

25. Twenty-year-old Enoch Ray was a private in Company A, Eighteenth Alabama Infantry. He was the oldest son of Margaret Ray, a widow from near Geneva, Alabama.

I went over to the 25th Regt. last Sunday. I found all of the boys well. There was seventeen on the sick list this morning.

If you see any chance, send me two boxes of your pills.

We hav plenty of water hear now.

I must close for the present. Give my love to all & kiss all of the children for me & give my respect to Mr. Beck and family.

> Nothin more at present.
> B. T. Moxley

~

[*Garret Stanley to William M. Moxley*]
Coffee County, Ala.
June 24th, 1862

G. Stanley of Coffee County, Ala., who was enlisted by W. M. Moxley to serve during the war, but by Reason of Disability was discharged from the service in January last. I hereby transfer any entire claim on the Confederate States to W. M. Moxley for value received. This, the 25th day of June, 1862.

> Garret Stanley
> his X mark
> Test,
> W. S. Justice

[*on same sheet: Julian Miller to William M. Moxley*]

Julian Miller of Coffee County, Ala., was enlisted by W. M. Moxley to serve during the war, but by Reason of Disability was discharged in February.

I hereby transfer my entire claim on the Confederate States this June 25, 1862.

> Julian Miller
> his X mark
> Test,
> W. S. Justice

～

[*T. E. E. Jackson to unidentified correspondent*]
[September 1863]

[*large fragment missing*] every day to get a chance to go to his company, which I made after so long a time, but the chance did me no good. After all, I will inform you immediatly after I find out the truth.

I hated very much to hear of so much sickness in Unkle Daniel's family. I hope they have all recovered before this time. I am very sorry to hear of so much sickness in that country, but few left there to till the land, & it seams as if they have to under go a serious power of sickness.

Tell Cousin Sousan that I am not able to give her any satisfaction concerning Lafayett. The last time I heard from him, he was at the hospital in Mississippi. I am very eager, indeed, to hear from him, myself. I fear some thing serious has happened to him. We are placed in such a condition here that we can not hear from each other very often. I will inform her immediately on learning the truth of the matter.

So, I will close as I want to drop a few lines to Mr. Stinson. Give my love to all. Save the same for yourself. Write soon. Nothing more, only to remain, as ever, yours truely,

Lieut. Jackson

T. E. E. Jackson

[*T. E. E. Jackson to Micajah B. Stinson on reverse of letter above*]
[September 1863]

Mr. M. B. Stinson

Sir,

I take this opportunity of droping you a few lines which, if you receive, will inform you that I am yet in the land & among the living, enjoying a reasonable portion of health, hoping that this may reach & find you & family the same.

The health of the company is good, viz., of what few is left of it. There is but twenty-four present now, since the fight, though there were but one killed dead on the field. It seams to me that the gap could not be filled by any two men that I know of. This was your Son, W[ilson] B. Stinson. He was killed on the 20th Sept. on the battle field of Chickamauga, about eleven o'Clock in the day. I am very sorry to say that I did not get to see him after we started into the fight. After

the charge was over & the storm had calmed, Sergt. [Robertus W.]
Reaves came to me and told me that Wilson was killed & that some
of our own regiment killed him. I was beat all over on receiving such
news. I wanted to go back & see him, but could not get the chance.
I have been informed by very good authority that he spoke a few
words after he was shot. A friend of his, who belongs to Co. H of the
regiment, was standing by him when he fell. As he fell he spoke &
said that he was killed, & that, too, by some of our own men. [*large
fragment missing*]

. . . to hear from you that you were well, but regret very much to
hear of your being in so much trouble about Jim & others of our
friends that come out badly in the fight. I am sorry to say that I am
not able to give you much satisfaction about Jim yet. I walked about
eight miles the other day to try to find out something concerning him,
but failed. I found the division that he belongs to, but his brigade was
off on picket where I could not get to them. So I had to come back
without learning anything of him whatever, which I hated very much.
No living person wants to find out the truth of his case worse than
[*remainder of letter missing*]

⌒

[*Appleton H. Justice to Conscription Authority*]
Bullock, Ala.
January 4, 1864

I hereby Certify that Doct. W. M. Moxley has been in the Practice
of Medicine for more than seven years & has never abandaned the
same & is now in the practice.

A. H. Justice
Sub-Enrolling Officer for Coffee County

⌒

[*Jourdan Beck to William M. Moxley*]
Pike County, Alabama
Feby. 8th, 1864
To Dr. W. M. Moxley

Dear Son,

These few lines will inform you that myself & family are all well
at this time, hoping they may find you & all well. I have nothing of

much interest to write, only Rob got home last night safe and well. He
brought us some letters. R[obertus] W. Reaves has been with us 5 or 6
days. He is well. J[os] went to carry him to Greenville & camped there,
& Rob went to the fire to warm & found him there, & thay came
home together. Burt's furlough was not out, but he wanted to go to
Ga. to see Linney. He only had 16 days furlough.

Mary and Tommy is well.[26] Our neighbors all well except W[ilson]
B. Stringer's darkeys. They have a hard time of it. There is several cases
on hand now. As some gets better, others are taken down. He says as
soon as they get so [*fragment missing*] he is going down there.

We have got no shoes for the children yet, nor George's Jeans. We
have had some fine weather lately. I killed my last hog last Thursday.
They weighed very well. Ja[mes]'s other hog weighed 270 lbs., which
will make him 555 lbs. I killed 2400 lbs. in all of my own.

I have not been to the [post] office since you left. I got one letter
from you by mail, and not a word from Mat since he left here. I have
wrote to him twice. I have not seen D. N[ewton Moxley] since you
left. Jos[eph] says there was 3 sacks of salt in Greenville for W[ilson]
B. [Stringer], 2 for Mat, & one for me. I had to borrow salt to salt my
meat.

Ellis was up last week after salt. He went to Hooks's to get some.
He got it. I dont know whether he bought or borrowed. I told him to
borrow, and I would stand security.

I have not been after the syrup yet. I thought I would wait untill
the salt came. I dont know when a waggon will go to Greenville, and
W. B.'s negroes keeps so sick.

Nelson has been down several days. He wants me to go, but I dont
know when to go. Hooks and J. B. [Joseph Stringer?] expect to get a
contract to make salt for the county.

Dr. McCarry[27] died last week of pneumonia.

The river is getting down now. If the bridges was up, we could cross
very well.

I dont know yet whether we will have any school at the Academy
this year or not.[28] There has been some efforts made, but the chance to

26. These are two of William Moxley's children, Mary Elizabeth and Davis, now renamed
Thompson.

27. William McCarra, aged fifty-four in 1860, was a Baptist minister from Troy, Alabama.

28. The Academy opened on what is now Academy Street in Troy, Alabama, in 1852 under Rev.
R. W. Priest. On 12 January 1864 the Troy *Southern Advertiser* called the attention of its readers to
the Academy. "Its principal, Mr. S. J. Doster, is a gentleman of long experience as an instructor of

get board is bad, as there is none of the neighbors likes to take in a boarder. Lusy has not come over yet.

I believe I cant think of any thing more worth writing, so I will try to close. We all join in sending our best respects to [*fragment missing*] Mat & Willy. The children all send houdy to you and Willy.

> I remain yours, as ever, & c.
> Jourdan Beck
> & family
> To
> W. M. Moxley
> M. L. Beck

~

[*Sarah E. Moxley Brooks to William M. Moxley*]
Traveler's Rest
[Louisville, Georgia]
March 28th, 1864
Dr. Wm M. Moxley

Dear Brother,

I embrace the present opportunity of writing you a short communication as I was not at home when your letter came for me or I would have answered it before now. I enjoyed my trip to Ala. very much, though I was sorry that I could not see you while I was out there. The children all were very glad to see me. I wish you would come out and bring them some time to see me. Clarisa came home with me and is here now.

Jasper is at home yet. I recon he will go before long. His health is a little better than it was when he first came home. [Benjamin] Thomas [Moxley] has got a detail to get cross ties on the rail road, so I dont recon he will have to go at all.

They have called out all from 17 to 50.[29] John Cheatham will have

---

youth, and has won an honorable distinction in his vocation. We can cheerfully recommend him to the public," wrote the editor. "Those desiring to place their children under an excellent instructor will find such an one in Mr. Doster." Farmer, *One Hundred Fifty Years in Pike County*, 201.

29. The Second Conscription Act, passed by the Confederate Congress in September 1862, and the Third Conscription Act, passed in February 1864, extended the ages of liability from seventeen to fifty. Moore, *Conscription and Conflict in the Confederacy*.

to go before long. I am looking for Newton to come every day. I received a letter from him last week, and he said he would come soon.

Jasper was very anxious to see you. If you just knew how bad he wanted to see you, I know you would have come to see him. He has been looking for you a good while. I do wish you would come.

This leaves us all in very good health, hoping to find you enjoy the same blessing. You must excuse this bad writing and short letter as I am in a hurry. Clarisa send her best regards to you and says if Johnnie is down there, tell him not to forget his promise, and she also sends her double and twisted love to him.

So, no more from your affectionate sister,
S. E. Brooks

~

[*Daniel Newton Moxley to William M. Moxley*]
New Providence
May the 3/1864
William M. Moxley

Dear Brother,

Yours of the 27 came to hand yesterday, which gave me mutch pleasure to hear that your health is improving. I cant tell how it is that you should accuse me of not wanting to correspond with you. I am shore that I have ansired all the letters that you have written me except the one that came by W. B. Stringer, and I should of ansired that if it had not been that I have bin engaged hunting those dezerters that was in this vasinity. I have bin so mutch interested in trying to bring them to justis that I have neglected all most every thing in way of business, and they are still unarested.[30]

I have no news of interest now. Mary Brooks[31] is here now and will stay sometime. She brout no news from Jefferson. Brother Joseph is at

---

30. After leaving the Twenty-fifth Alabama, Daniel Newton Moxley received a commission from Governor Thomas Hill Watts to suppress the depredations of deserters in south Alabama. *Memorial Record of Alabama*, 1:788–789; Martin, *Desertion of Alabama Troops from the Confederate Army*.

31. Mary I. Brooks is William's and Newton's niece, the daughter of their sister Sarah E. Brooks.

home, & I sopose that his health is still bad. I wish you could asist him
in som way to get him out of the servis.

I went to Troy[32] sometime ago to see about your case, and when
they found out that the case would be fully envistigated, and Mrs.
Bryant went up and payed up the [*word illegible*] and dismissed the
case. I cant tell what she will do now.

You wrote to me that if I was down thare you could fix me up so
that the Conscript could not interfere with me.[33] I want you to write
me soon as you can, and I will come down as soon as I can. I cant
leave now. Thar is more pushing [and] shoving than you ever saw to
git details.

I want you to write to me all about the matter what I shall have to
do and how I shall [*word illegible*] prepaired.

I resieved a letter som time ago from James L. Little. He said that
he wanted to correspond with me so that he could hear from us
acusionlly.

> I must com to a close.
> Yours, as ever,
> D. N. Moxley

⁓

[*Robertus W. Reeves to Editor*, Southern Advertiser, *Troy, Alabama*]
Near Atlanta, Aug. 8, 1864

Mr. Editor:

I send you a list of casualties in Co. B, 25th Ala. Reg., which you
will please publish for the benefit of the friends of the killed and
wounded.

Killed: W. J. Brunson, Joshua Andrews, T. J. Ward, G. E. Wise.

Wounded: R. W. Reeves, in head slight; B. R. Brunson, in hip leg
and arm; R. M. Brunson, thigh broke; J. Cubstid, arm slight; G. W.
Hall, in bowels, since dead; J. E. Holmes, in thigh; E. Nelson, in thigh;
J. W. Ray, chin, severely; J. W. Moore, in arm; L. B. Johnson, breast
slight; F. G. Underwood, head; N. Pick, leg; J. B. Moore, in leg.

---

32. Troy, Alabama, was the seat of Pike County.

33. For a discussion of exemptions from military service in Alabama, see Fleming, *Civil War and
Reconstruction in Alabama*, 100–108.

The Company left the county under Capt. Curtis, the 1st day of September, 1861, and has participated in all the fights with Gen. Bragg's army from Shiloh.

Yesterday the enemy shelled our pickets heavily and then threw a skirmish line forward, but they were soon repulsed. It is the fourth time they have tried our pickets on this part of the line. Everything is quiet today except an occasional shot from the enemy's artillery.

> R. W. Reeves
> O[rderly] S[ergeant], Co. B, 25th Ala. Regt.

~

[*Joseph Brannon to William M. Moxley*]
Nov. 28th, 1864
Camp near Opelika, Ala.

Sir,

Acording to promis, I seat my self to drop you a few lines to inform you that I am well & harty at the present, hoping these few lines may reach you in due time & find you & famly in the best of helth.

Well, Dr., I have nothing of importance to wright to you at this time. I recht my command safe an sound [*word illegible*] I was not [*word illegible*] not [*word illegible*] way on the road 14 days. The command left Oxford the day before I got there. I followed after them & over toock them at this place. I found the boys all well. I dont think we will stay here long, but I dont know where we will go to, but I think we will go to Mississippi when we leave hear.

Dr., I hav no war nuse to wright to you. We git no neuse hear. The boys ar in good spirits hear.

Dr., I want you to assist J. H. Justice in getting my Detail papers, that is, if it can be don. The company oficers is vary ancious for me to remain at home to work in the shop, & you know the condition of our contry, & it makes me more ancious to git back thar than any thing else.

So, I will close. Expecting to hear from you so[o]n & often. Direct to Joseph Brannon, Co. D, 6 Ala. Calvry, C. S. Lee, Capt., Opelika, Ala.[34]

34. Recruited from Barbour, Coffee, Coosa, Henry, Macon, Montgomery, Pike, and Tallapoosa Counties, the Sixth Alabama Cavalry was organized near Pine Level, early in 1863, as part of Brig.

Nothing more, onley I still remain your friend, as ever,
Joseph Brannon[35]

~

[*John B. Curtis to William M. Moxley*]
New Providence
Decbr. 17/64

Dr. W. M. Moxley,

Our Mutual friend & Bro., J. L. Stinson, died to day. We will bury him Masonically tomorrow at 3 Oclock P. M. We wish all the Bullock Lodge to join us. Please come & bring aprons &c.

Fraternally Yours,
J. B. Curtis[36]

Gen. James H. Clanton's brigade. Its first duty station was Pollard, from which it observed Union forces at Pensacola. It served briefly near Decatur, Alabama, and was then attached to the Army of Tennessee for the Atlanta campaign. Thereafter it returned to the Florida panhandle until it was called upon to help resist Maj. Gen. James H. Wilson's raid into Alabama in 1865. The regiment laid down its arms at Gainesville, Florida, with the end of the war. C. H. Colvin of Pike County served as the regiment's only colonel. The Coffee County company was commanded by Capt. C. S. Lee, Jr.

35. Pvt. Joseph Brannon, Company D, Sixth Alabama Cavalry, was formerly a private in Moxley's company. A forty-four-year-old farmer from Coffee County in 1860, he was married with four children.

36. William Moxley was a member of the Bullock Masonic Lodge in Coffee County, and John L. Stinson and Micajah B. Stinson were both members of the Troy Masonic Lodge 56 in Pike County. "East Troy Masonic Lodge Membership Roster," http://www.intersurf.com/~johnjanr/masonic.htm.

8

"A prettie wild country"

6 September 1870–20 April 1891

By 6 September 1870, William Moxley was living at Lone Oak in Hunt County, Texas, with his second wife, Martha E. (Justice) Moxley—the widow of Dr. Sidney A. Warren—and his children, George Edwin, Mary Elizabeth, Laura, William Jasper, Davis (now renamed Thompson), and a new baby, Appleton Justice, born in Texas on 14 March 1869.[1] There he continued to practice medicine and was a partner, with Walter P. Bush, in the Moxley and Bush Drug Store.

William Morel Moxley seems to have died in December 1878, for on 16 December, his widow was named administrator of his estate, and on the thirtieth day of that month she purchased burial plot number eighty-eight in the Greenville, Texas, cemetery. Moxley was listed on both the Hunt County tax roles and the role of physicians in Hunt

---

1. As a result of the destruction of the Coffee County courthouse on 3 September 1863, the date and place of Moxley's marriage to Martha E. (Justice) Warren cannot now be determined.

Their only child, Appleton Justice Moxley, died on 27 September 1877 and is buried in the East Mount Cemetery, Greenville, Texas. 1870 Census of the United States, Hunt County, Texas, p. 394; *Early Birth Records, Hunt County, Texas, 1873–1876: Physicians in Hunt County, Texas, 1842–1906* (Commerce, Tex.: D. J. Associates, 1984), 17; Robert Lee Thompson and Kathy Lynn Penson, comps., *Cemetery Inscriptions of Hunt County, Texas* (St. Louis, Mo.: Frances Terry Ingmire, 1979), 3:64.

County for 1878, but the following year he was missing, and his widow was listed as the owner of what had been his property.[2]

To Martha E. Moxley he left, "for last years' support," one hundred and fifty acres of land, $266.55 in cash and unpaid accounts, household and kitchen furniture worth $150.00, two horses and a wagon valued at $50.00, a buggy worth $30.00, two mules valued at $100.00, nine head of cattle worth $45.00, and two hogs worth $10.00.

Following William Moxley's death, his widow was married for a third time on 15 December 1880 to Z. W. Davidson of Hunt County, Texas, and, as they came of age, his remaining children scattered across west Texas and the Indian Nation, now Oklahoma. As the older generation died off, Mary Verlinda E. (Beck) Stinson alone remained in the valley of the Conecuh River and attempted to maintain communication with her sister's son's and daughters.

[*Mary Verlinda E. (Beck) Stinson to George E. Moxley*]
Henderson, Ala., June 6th, 1877
Mr. G. E. Moxley,

Dear George,

Your very welcome letter has been recd. As usual, was glad to hear from you & was very glad indeed to get your picture, although you have changed so much I would not have known you. The health of our family [is] just tolerably good. Pa's health [is] not better than when I wrote you last.[3] Joe's wife and babe not well, having the chills. Neighbors genrally well. I hear of some sickness on the other side of the river. The Dr.'s [Daniel Newton Moxley] family well. Pa & Joe are gone over there today to go driving with the Dr. I got a letter from

2. Since family letters dated as late as 1891 indicate that his grave remained unmarked, and since his infant son, Appleton Justice Moxley, who died in 1877, only a year before his father, is buried in the East Mount Cemetery, we may perhaps safely infer that William M. Moxley, too, is buried there in a grave now lost. Probate Court Records, Hunt County, Texas, vol. B, pp. 366, 370, 377, 378, 415, 416, 432, 455, 531, 582, and vol. C, pp. 10 and 86. Index of Deeds, Hunt County, Texas, Book M, p. 14, and Book Y, p. 130; *Hunt County Marriages, 1846–1911* (Greenville, Tex.: Hunt County Genealogical Society, 1987), 335.

3. Jourdan Beck died on 7 March 1878, twelve years after his wife, Elizabeth Beck, who died on 23 August 1866 at the age of fifty-six. Both are buried in the Spears Cemetery.

Mollie Gilpin. All well with her & well pleased with their new home. Have good prospects for a crop. Crops in this section are very small, & most of the farmers up with their work & waiting for rain so they can commence laying by corn. We are needing rain very bad. Almost four weeks since we had any. The river in very good order for fishing. We had a fish fry one day last week. Got more than we could eat for dinner. I wish you had been with us. We are thinking of having one next Saturday if it does not rain.

Grandma Williamson[4] is dead. Mr. Pouney[?] (the old preacher) is very low down if not dead. Mr. Louis Horn[?] very sick. I hear of [a] good deal of sickness in the vicinity of Troy. Mrs. Tullis has been very sick.

Our little school will be out in about three weeks. Emma is getting tired of going [to a] school so small and no larger scholars. She gets very lonesome. Mr. Bricken in Bullock will have an examination & exhibition the first day of July. He has a very good school.

Rossie & myself went to Troy last week. I have not seen the place since the war & would not have known it, [there] has been such great improvement since that time.

I got a letter from Cousin Emiline [Stinson]. All well with her. Cousin Bent[?] is teaching school. Has from 60 to 70 students. Dr. Stringer's health still bad, but some better than it has been.

Tell Laura, Emma is getting [*word illegible*] with her for not writing. She has been looking for a letter from her for some time. Tell her she must write. Also, Willie, too. Give them my love. Tell Bettie I have a very nice garden; been having beans some time. My love to her & family. Tell Buddie[5] I want to see him, & he must send me his picture. I would be so proud of it. You have him to get one taken & send to me. Tell him to write to me.

Well, George, I suppose you think my letter very simple. I write to you as though you were still a child. When I look at your picture I can hardly realize that it is the shadow of my little George. You look to[o] manly. You have no idea how I appreciate your picture. I will send

4. Abigail Williamson was the mother of Margaret Ann Stringer, the mother-in-law of Wilson Stringer, and the grandmother of Mary M. Stringer. Mary Stringer was married to Mary Beck Stinson's brother, Matthew Allen Beck, and therefore would, by courtesy, become "Grandma" to all of the family.

5. In January 1891, Thompson Davis Moxley, as he called himself, but "Buddie" to his family, moved to Oakland, Indian Territory, to become a farmer.

you mine when I get the chance to have one taken. Excuse this short, uninteresting scribble. Let me hear from you soon.

Yours, with much love,
M. V. E. Stinson

~

[*William Jasper Moxley to George E. Moxley*]
Tascosa, Texas
April 24, [18]84
Mr. G. E. Moxley[6]

Dear Brother,

Your most welcome [letter] came to hand a few minutes ago. Was glad to hear from you & to know that you and family were well. This leaves me injo[y]ing the same good health. We are have[ing] some of the finest weather now that I ever saw, for the time a year. I believe horses & cattle are looking well.

Well, George, I would not care if I was down there for a while. This is getting to be a prettie wild country now. There has been a bout 15 Mexicans killed here since Christmas, and some cow boys. This is getting to be a bout as bad as San Antonio used to be, between the cow boys & Mexicans. There is two companys of Mexicans here now. New Mexico is arming them, and they are cause[ing] trouble in this country, I am a fraid, but after this spring, things will be quiet & times will be better.

Well, George, as I have nothing of interest to write, will close by asking you to write soon. Give my love to all the family.

As ever,
W. J. Moxley

P.S. George, let me know at what time you want that money. I can send it any time after the first of the year.

As ever, W. J. Moxley[7]

6. George E. Moxley married Allie W. Morris in Lone Oak, a village in southeastern Hunt County, Texas, on 15 September 1878. He died in Midland, Anderson County, Texas, 22 February 1937. *Hunt County Marriages, 1846–1911,* 335; Texas state Department of Health, Bureau of Vital Statistics, Certificate of Death Number 6033.

7. By 1884 William Jasper Moxley was cattle ranching in Tascosa, Texas. He died in Andrews

~

[*Mary Elizabeth (Moxley) Featherson to George E. Moxley*]
[8 June 1890
Whittville, Comanche County, Texas]

George and Allie Moxley
Dear Bro. and Sister,

As the children are writing, I will rite a few lines. I received a letter
from Aunt Mollie [Mary Verlinda] Stinson not long ago. She is thinking hard of you for not writing to her. Uncle Tom Moxley is dead.
Uncle Newton drinks a grate deal of his time. He has four children
living. George, if I ask you one question, will you answer it? Do you
drink? Now, don't think hard of me for asking the question. I hafe won-
dered a many a time if one of my three brothers did use the stuff.

George, I want you to write me a long letter and tell me all the
newes and tell me all a bout the kinfolks. Moxley and Emily[8] a[re] so
glad to get a letter from you and Allie. They have several corspondance.

George, I would be glad if you could move out here. I am satisfied a
work man could do well here. There is so manny buildings going up in
Comanche, and Brownwood is a considerable city. We live in 18 miles
of Brownwood & 12 miles of Comanche. I [k]no[w] if you could visit
our country you would like it there. Ed is trying to sell every day. We
want to [be near] a good school.

I will close. Hope to here from you. My love to all. Kiss the children for me.

Your devoted sister,
Bettie Featherson

County, Texas, 30 October 1931. Texas state Department of Health, Bureau of Vital Statistics, Certificate of Death Number 45262.

8. Mary J. Elizabeth Moxley married Edward B. Featherson in Hunt County, Texas, on 27 October 1874 and later farmed cotton in Comanche, Texas. Moxley and Emily are their children and
would, of course, have been the grandchildren of William and Emily Moxley. *Hunt County Marriages, 1846–1911, 335.*

~

[*Mary Elizabeth (Moxley) Featherson to George E. Moxley*]
Comanche, Texas
Jan. 23, [18]91

Dear Broather,

I received your most wellcom letter some time a go which gave me much pleasure to read. This leaves all well at present. I hope this will find you all well. We have had some verry *cold* weather. Two snows in this month. Ed has not got off yet. The weather has ben so bad he don't know when he will get off. He will make a crop up there if he gets there in time.

January the 26

Ed started this morning. Left us all in tears. He will be gone till after cotton planting. Field went with him. I did not no how well I loved him untill he is gone a while.

George, I have not [heard] a word from Will and Buddie since I was there. I wrote to them when I got home and got no answer. I receaved a letter from Sis [Mary Verlinda E. Beck Stinson] and Emma the other day. Sis wants us five to buy a stone to put on Ma's grave. I think Pa's grave is first, as Ma's is marked by relatives. If you will see the other children, [find out] what they will do and let me [k]no[w]. I will do a little more than they will. I had rather you would not ask Ma [Martha E. (Justice) Moxley?] to do anny thing toward fixing Pa's grave. There is nine of us, and I think we can fix the grave. Find out what each one will give, and let me [k]no[w] as soon as you can. I can't give anny thing to Sis untill Pa's is fixt up. I will send you Sis's letter. You need [not] send it to Will untill you speak to him a bout Pa's grave.

So good by. Rite soon.

Love to all,
Bettie Featherston

~

[*Mary Verlinda E. Beck Stinson to George E. Moxley*]
Fleetwood, Ala., April 20, 1891
Mr. G. E. Moxley,

Dear Nephew,

  Your very welcome letter came to hand in due time. I was very
glad to hear from you once more & to hear you were well & getting
along well. You say you have a good little place. I would advise you to
stay on it & quit moveing so much. Remember the old story: a rolling
stone will gather no moss. We are getting along very well. Made very
good crops last year. Have some of our cotton on hand yet. Been holding it for a better price. Sold some last week for 7¼, so we have not
gained any thing by holding.

  Our neighbors are generaly well and getting tolerably well. We have
had a cold, wet spring. Corn all got killed down the first of this month,
but is coming out. Have some cotton up. Garden sorry.

  A negro got drowned in the river above here last Saturday. He was
drinking and started to swim across and sunk. A crowd worked nearly
all day yesterday hunting his body, but did not find it.

  A crowd calling themselves White Caps are doing some depredations around here. They [went] to a negro's house on Mrs. Warren's
place last Saturday night & shot in & under & around the house &
left a note for him giving him ten days to leave or they would repeat
the dose. Fortunately, the negroes were not at home. If they had been,
I expect someone would have got killed. They have been going to
some other places, running negroes from their homes.

  Well, we will soon have a rail road near us. One is being built from
Troy down the river on the other side. It crosses the road at the old
Reaves place. Will have a depot there.[9]

  Joe [Beck][10] has bought a business lot & a residence lot. He thinks
of moving over there. He is getting along very well, making some
money. He and Dr. [Newton] Moxley has a steam saw mill over there
on the R. R. doing a good business. The Dr. drinks a good deal yet,
but is getting along well. His oldest son is married & has one child.

  Well, George, I wrote to Bettie about having your Ma's grave fixed,

---

9. The "old Reaves place" was at present Glenwood, Alabama, in what was then Pike County.
10. Joseph J. Beck died on 11 September 1926 and is buried beside his wife, Mattie E. Beck, in
the Friendship Baptist Church Cemetery at Bullock.

but she said she was not able to do any thing for it now. I wish you all were able to get a tomb for her grave. I have some at Pa's, Ma's, & Lafayette's, & I want your Ma and brother Tom's fixed.[11]

My health is bad all the time. Emma has been in bad health about two years. She has four children, two boys & two girls, all going to school but the baby. The school will close next Friday.

George, I want you to write often. I love to get your letters. Tell me how many children you have and their names. Give my love to your wife & and children & accept a large share for your dear self.

Write soon to your affectionate
Aunt M. V. E. Stinson[12]

11. Although we cannot now determine who marked Emily A. M. Moxley's grave and when, her gravestone matches those of her father, mother, brother Charles A. Thompson Beck, and sister, Mary Verlinda E. Stinson, beside whom she is buried.

12. Mary Verlinda E. Stinson remained in the Henderson area for the rest of her life. In 1921 she applied for a Confederate pension. Her address then was Glenwood, Crenshaw County, Alabama. She died there on 18 February 1932 and is buried at the Spears Cemetery between her mother and her sister Emily.

Bibliography

Manuscripts

Clanton's Brigade: Dubose Manuscript. Alabama Department of Archives and History, Montgomery, Alabama. [Available online at homepages.rootsweb. com/~ddfedrd/dubose.html.]

Confederate Muster Rolls Collection, Alabama Department of Archives and History, Montgomery, Alabama.

Probate Court Records, Hunt County, Texas, Volume B. Texas State Library and Archives, Austin, Texas.

Books

Primary Sources

Avary, Myrta Lockett, ed. *A Virginia Girl in the Civil War, 1861–1865: Being a Record of the Actual Experiences of the Wife of a Confederate Officer.* New York: D. Appleton, 1903.

Beck, Brandon H., ed. *"Third Alabama!": The Civil War Memoir of Brigadier General Cullen Andrews Battle, CSA.* Tuscaloosa: University of Alabama Press, 1999.

Burr, Virginia Ingraham, ed. *The Secret Eye: The Journal of Ella Gertrude Clanton Thomas, 1848–1889.* Chapel Hill: University of North Carolina Press, 1990.

Clay-Clopton, Virginia. *A Belle of the Fifties: Memoirs of Mrs. Clay of Alabama.* Edited by Leah Rawls Atkins, Joseph H. Harrison, Jr., and Sara A. Hudson. Tuscaloosa: University of Alabama Press, 1999.

Estes, Claude, comp. *List of Field Officers, Regiments and Battalions in the Confederate States Army, 1861–1865.* Macon, Ga.: J. W. Burke, 1912.

Henderson, Lillian, comp. *Roster of the Confederate Soldiers of Georgia, 1861–1865.* 4 vols. Hapeville, Ga.: Longino and Porter, 1959–1964.

Jones, Edgar W. *History of the 18th Alabama Infantry Regiment-CSA.* Edited by Zane Geier. 2 vols. Birmingham, Ala.: C. D. A. Pulcrano, 1994. [Available online at http://www.looksmart.com/r?page=/search/frames/index.html&isp= US&name=&bcolor=ffccoo&key=edgar+W.+Jones+alabama&url=http%3a// www.hueytown.com/historical/Military/Military%2520Subjects.htm&pskip= &nskip=10&se=0,0,0,933&index=1.]

Lord, Walter, ed. *The Fremantle Diary.* Boston: Little, Brown, 1954.

Richardson, James D., ed. *A Compilation of the Messages and Papers of the Confederacy Including the Diplomatic Correspondence, 1861–1865.* 2 vols. Nashville: United States Publishing, 1906.

Sifkas, Stewart, comp. *Compendium of the Confederate Armies: South Carolina and Georgia.* New York: Facts on File, 1995.

U.S. Navy Department. *The War of the Rebellion: A Compilation of the Official Records of the Union and Confederate Navies.* 30 vols. Washington, D.C., 1894–1922.

U.S. War Department. *Revised Regulations for the Army of the United States, 1861.* Philadelphia: J. G. L. Brown, 1861.

———. *The War of the Rebellion: A Compilation of the Official Records of the Union and Confederate Armies.* 128 vols. Washington, D.C., 1880–1901.

Secondary Sources

Alabama Civil War Centennial Commission. *Brief Historical Sketches of Military Organization Raised in Alabama During the Civil War: Reproduced from Willis Brewer's "Alabama: Her History, Resources, War Record, and Public Men, From 1540 to 1872."* University, Ala.: Alabama Civil War Centennial Commission, 1962.

Bergeron, Arthur W., Jr. *Confederate Mobile.* Jackson: University Press of Mississippi, 1991.

Bleser, Carol, ed. *In Joy and Sorrow: Women, Family, and Marriage in the Victorian South, 1830–1890.* New York: Oxford University Press, 1991.

Brewer, Willis. *Alabama: Her History, Resources, War Record, and Public Men,*

From 1540 to 1872. 1872. Rept. Baltimore: Clearfield, 1995. [Available online at http://www.archives.state.al.us/referenc/alamilor/mil_org.html.]

Brooks, Stewart. *Civil War Medicine.* Springfield, Ill.: Charles C. Thomas, 1966.

Censer, Jane Turner. *North Carolina Planters and Their Children, 1800–1860.* Baton Rouge: Louisiana State University Press, 1984.

Clinton, Catherine, and Nina Silber, eds. *Divided Houses: Gender and the Civil War.* New York: Oxford University Press, 1992.

Cooling, Benjamin Franklin. *Forts Henry and Donelson: The Key to the Confederate Heartland.* Knoxville: University of Tennessee Press, 1987.

Cunningham, Horace H. *Doctors in Gray.* Baton Rouge: Louisiana State University Press, 1958.

Daniel, Larry J. *Shiloh: The Battle That Changed the Civil War.* New York: Simon and Schuster, 1997.

Davis, William C. *Battle at Bull Run.* New York: Doubleday, 1977.

Farmer, Margaret Pace. *One Hundred Fifty Years in Pike County, Alabama, 1821–1971.* Anniston, Ala.: Higginbotham, 1973.

Faust, Drew Gilpin. *Mothers of Invention: Women of the Slaveholding South in the American Civil War.* Chapel Hill: University of North Carolina Press, 1996.

Fleming, Walter L. *Civil War and Reconstruction in Alabama.* New York: Macmillan, 1905.

Fox-Genovese, Elizabeth. *Within the Plantation: Black and White Women of the Old South.* Chapel Hill: University of North Carolina Press, 1988.

Haythornthwaite, Philip J. *The Armies of Wellington.* London: Brockhampton Press, 1994.

Hughes, Nathaniel Cheairs, Jr., and Roy P. Stonesifer. *The Life and Wars of Gideon J. Pillow.* Chapel Hill: University of North Carolina Press, 1993.

Logue, Mickey, and Jack Simms. *Auburn . . . the loveliest village: A Pictorial History.* Norfolk, Va.: Donning, 1981.

McDonough, James Lee. *Shiloh: In Hell Before Night.* Knoxville: University of Tennessee Press, 1977.

McMillan, Malcolm C. *The Disintegration of a Confederate State: Three Governors and Alabama's Wartime Home Front, 1861–1865.* Macon, Ga.: Mercer University Press, 1986.

McMillen, Sally G. *Motherhood in the Old South: Pregnancy, Childbirth, and Infant Rearing.* Baton Rouge: Louisiana State University Press, 1990.

McPherson, James M. *Battle Cry of Freedom: The Civil War Era.* New York: Oxford University Press, 1988.

McWhiney, Grady. *Braxton Bragg and the Confederate Defeat: Field Command.* New York: Columbia University Press, 1969.

Martin, Bessie. *Desertion of Alabama Troops from the Confederate Army: A Study in Sectionalism.* New York: Columbia University Press, 1932.

Memorial Record of Alabama: A Concise Account of the State's Political, Military, Professional and Industrial Progress, together with the Personal Memoirs of Many of its People. Madison, Wisc.: Brant and Fuller, 1893.

Moore, Albert Burton. *Conscription and Conflict in the Confederacy.* New York: Macmillan, 1924.

Newton, Steven H. *Joseph E. Johnston and the Defense of Richmond.* Lawrence: University Press of Kansas, 1999.

Owen, Thomas McAdory. *History of Alabama and Dictionary of Alabama Biography.* 4 vols. Chicago: S. J. Clarke, 1921.

Rogers, William Warren, Robert David Ward, Leah Rawls Atkins, and Wayne Flynt. *Alabama: The History of a Deep South State.* Tuscaloosa: University of Alabama Press, 1994.

Steiner, Paul E. *Disease in the Civil War: Natural Biological Warfare in 1861–1865.* Springfield, Ill.: Charles C. Thomas, 1968.

Sterkx, H. E. *Partners in Rebellion: Alabama Women in the Civil War.* Rutherford, N.J.: Fairleigh Dickinson University Press, 1970.

Stewart, John Craig. *The Governors of Alabama.* Gretna, La.: Pelican Publishing, 1975.

Sword, Wiley. *Shiloh: Bloody April.* New York: William Morrow, 1974.

Watson, Fred S. *Coffee Grounds: A History of Coffee County Alabama, 1841–1970.* 1970. Rept. Enterprise, Ala.: Pea River Historical and Genealogy Society, 1985.

Wheeler, Joseph. *Alabama. Confederate Military History, Extended Ed.,* vol. 8, edited by Clement A. Evans. Wilmington, N.C.: Broadfoot Publishing, 1987.

Wiley, Bell I. *The Life of Johhny Reb.* Indianapolis: Bobbs-Merrill, 1943.

Williams, L. B. *A Sketch of the 33rd Alabama Volunteer Infantry Regiment and Its Role in Cleburne's Elite Division of the Army of Tennessee, 1862–1865.* Auburn, Ala.: L. B. Williams, 1990.

Articles

Faust, Drew Gilpin. "Altars of Sacrifice: Confederate Women and the Narratives of War." *Journal of American History* 76:4 (March 1990), 1200–1228.

Hallock, Judith Lee. "'Lethal and Debilitating': The Southern Disease Environment as a Factor in Confederate Defeat." *Journal of Confederate History* 7 (1991), 51–61.

Krug, Donna Rebecca D. "Women and War in the Confederacy." In *On the Road to Total War: The American Civil War and the German Wars of Unification, 1861–1871,* edited by Stig Förster and Jörg Nagler. New York: Cambridge University Press, 1997.

McMillan, Malcolm C. "Alabama." In *The Confederate Governors,* edited by W. Buck Yearns. Athens: University of Georgia Press, 1985.

Index